GOD

God Can Do It Here!

Eileen Vincent

Marshalls

Marshalls Paperbacks
Marshall Morgan & Scott

1 Bath Street, London EC1V 9LB

First published by Marshall Morgan & Scott 1982

ISBN : 0 551 01011 8

Printed in Great Britain by Hunt Barnard Printing, Aylesbury

The cover:
A flood of people

I drew the picture (reproduced on the front cover of this book) to describe something God showed me 2 years ago at the New Forest Fellowship holiday.

It was the day the rain fell in torrents. Many of us were at a barbecue in the marquee. Occasionally, through the doorways one could see this tremendous downpour. Suddenly the word spread that while we were eating and drinking, tents and caravans were being flooded out!

From a bird's eye view we must have looked like ants scurrying from their damaged nest. Pandemonium broke out as people dashed about, sorting out all the problems. However, in this 'crisis' God achieved more in bringing us together than He would otherwise have done in the whole week on the campsite. Coping with all the problems was very hard work but when everything was done there was such a feeling of elation in the camp. Although things had seemed chaotic and crazy, it turned out to be a most glorious day!

The Lord then showed me that He is going to 'rain people' down on us in the same way – like torrential rain; every raindrop will be a person. The 'smallest to the greatest' will have to plunge into the work that follows, for thousands will be falling around us, needing and wanting Jesus Christ.

My thoughts went back to this on the last Sunday of 1981 in Bedmond when Eileen prayed the following prayer. One doesn't usually take down people's prayers, but the Lord simply told me to 'listen to this prayer'. As I listened I knew I must illustrate the vision and share it with you. It is relevant to the year ahead and I hope it blesses you all.

Janet Bennett

Just by raindrops

Eileen's 'Snowflake Prayer'

Lord – I was impressed afresh
In the way all things You do
Seem to be done by little bits
Added together;
Just as the snow falls
And covers the whole earth
Around us – all just little flakes.
The whole district can get wet
Just by raindrops!

Lord – I want to praise You
When I think
That Your church can be filled
Just by 'ones'.
And Lord, come next Christmas
What can we expect?
What shall we hope for?
What shall we look for
From You, Father?

Lord – if You can just
Open the heavens
And so many snowflakes,
Individual ones, fall down
And the whole earth is covered –
Lord, what could You do
Amongst us?!

Oh Father – my heart
Lifts up to You.
You deal with individuals.
You always deal with the small thing
But intend it to be great and big,
Full and mature.
Lord – we look for growth,
One by one.
Oh, give us a heart of expectancy,
An attitude of work Lord,
Within us.

Lord – add to us.
Cause us to grow.
Cause us to put on one side
Our desires for smallness –
That smallness Father, that was
Put to death
When You went to the cross
To die
For the whole world,
Not for just a handful.
May we have the same heart
As Jesus.

Eileen Vincent

Contents

List of photographs

Foreword

My brothers and sisters in England,

It's my great pleasure to have the opportunity of writing a foreword for your book 'God Can Do It Here'.

Jesus Christ is the same yesterday, today, and forever (Heb. 13:8). He is the same both in England and Korea. It goes without saying that it can also happen in England. All you have to do is to move the hands of God by constant prayer in a firm faith in Jesus Christ. He is alive! He performs miracles; He heals the sick; He comforts the despondent and depressed; He gives us the wisdom of God, and He solves every problem by His almighty power.

There are many diseases beyond medical care but there is no disease God cannot heal. There are so many problems arising beyond human knowledge but there is none He cannot solve. What a thrill and joy to experience the almighty power of God! The power of Jesus Christ! The power of the Holy Spirit!

Then how can we move the hands of God? In the first place, we should believe in Jesus Christ our Saviour, and that by His almighty power, He performs miracles upon those who believe in Him (Matt. 11:25). He never performs miracles upon those who doubt His miraculous power.

Secondly, we should pray constantly (I Thess. 5:17); prayer is the key to everything.

Thirdly, we should accept the Holy Spirit. We should recognise the Holy Spirit, and we should welcome the Holy Spirit. St Paul says in Acts 19:2, 'Have you received the Holy Spirit since you believed?'

The Holy Spirit is the Spirit of God, the Spirit of Jesus Christ, and Jesus Christ is the Way, the Truth, and the

Life, just like the Word of God is. He is the Word.

Christianity is beyond philosophy, beyond human logic. Jesus Christ is the only way to successful living, happiness and everything that is good, even unto everlasting life.

Sure it can happen also in England. Just move the hands of God.

May God bless you all in England.

Dr Paul Yonggi Cho, D.D., D.Litt.
Full Gospel Central Church

Preface

This book makes no attempt to be a complete survey of the work of God in Korea, where many remarkable things are happening. My purpose here is only to present my personal experience of Full Gospel Central Church, the biggest in the world.

In these pages I have expressed the deepest feelings of my heart which I know are shared by many others. To some they may sound extravagant but may I ask you to have patience and faith as we wait for God to do a wonder.

The names throughout the book are authentic. The frequent mention of Lee is simply because there are far more Lee's in Korea than Jones's in Wales.

The references are from the Revised Standard Version throughout except where indicated.

Thank-you's

The thank-you list for this book is going to be the longest ever. Although I actually did the writing it is the result of a huge collective effort of a most wonderful church to whom I express my deepest thanks.

Joy did my housework, others baked cakes, Jean's extra sitting room provided me with a quiet sanctuary away from the phone and people. At least half a dozen typists came to my aid but especially Ruth who doggedly typed the first copy and Gill who spent a week of her holiday doing the final manuscript. Then I must thank three Peters, one who carefully drew the map and graph, another for checking my references and Peter Inchley for his valuable comments and reading of the final manuscript.

My thanks spread to the other side of the world to the wonderful people I met at Full Gospel Central Church. Especially Pastor Cho for giving me the privilege of spending time in his church and Pastor Lee for being such an outstanding encouragement.

Lastly my special thanks go to my family and most of all to Alan, my husband, who has believed in me. He has been my principle inspiration and support, without which this would never have been written.

ONE

Seeing is believing

I opened my eyes and felt suddenly wide awake. 'What's that noise?' I said to Alan. A glance at the clock told me it was only six thirty a.m., but the room was light. Quickly jumping out of bed I opened the curtains. The most amazing sight confronted me. We stared down from our bedroom window at a sea of heads, nearly all black-haired, milling about below. The people were so crammed we could hardly see their bodies.

The noise I had heard was thousands and thousands of people waiting in the cool morning air to get into Seoul's vast Full Gospel Central Church. The first service of the day began at seven a.m. The atmosphere was one of excitement, singing from loud speakers filling the air and the low buzz of voices all chattering at once was mixed with the roar of busy traffic. The road, six lanes wide, was alive with green taxis like dodgem cars, all looking for a space to stop. Doors flew open and out tumbled mums and dads with children on all sides. Everywhere streams of people were pouring from buses or through the large barricades, all hurrying, even running to join the sea of people going slowly and orderly up the long flight of steps into the main auditorium.

When we had arrived the night before the place was almost deserted, just a few parked cars in what had seemed to be a huge car park in front of the impressive church buildings. Now I could see that the open space was not primarily a car park but necessary to accommodate the massive congregation.

Before we came to Korea we had looked at photographs of the huge church that Dr Yonggi Cho had established in Seoul, but to see the same view with our own eyes and to feel the electric atmosphere filled us with awe. As we gazed down from our ninth floor vantage point in the World Mission Building adjacent to the main auditorium, we were praising God, holding back our tears, swept over by deep emotions: God was in this place. Scrambling to get our clothes on quickly, we felt frustrated that we had been sleeping whilst important things were happening.

An army of 10,000

Some months earlier the seed thought of visiting Korea had been born in Alan's heart. It became a link in a chain of events. At home in the Watford district of Hertfordshire we suffer from the activities of many false cults, some of which have their headquarters in this locality. One day when Alan was driving past the Hare Krishna centre he saw large crowds; they were holding a special meeting. Indignation rose in his heart. Here in the Hertfordshire countryside were saffron-robed men with shaven heads and women in drab saris with little children in tow, all come to worship Hindu gods. With a sprinkling of respectability and a cloak of intellectual pride, Hinduism was being pushed as acceptable. Alan's indignation turned to anger. We had been missionaries in India and knew what the worship of idols did to the people. He cried out to God, 'Lord, if I had an army of 10,000 I would surround that place with praying people and drive out those deceiving spirits.'

Monthly we come together as a whole church for intercession. These are times when we believe God to break the powers of darkness in our area so that we shall see people being saved and the church built. At one of these prayer meetings Alan was musing in his heart on the thought of an army of 10,000. (Christians who would not obey or whose first interest was their success, independently fighting their own little wars, could never fulfil God's purpose on earth even if there were 10,000 of them.) It had to be an army, 10,000 people ready for war, trained, obedient, each knowing his place and function. He longed to pray out his heart's desire but thought, 'No it's unrealistic. What if it doesn't happen?' His mind was whirling with unbelieving thoughts when a word of prophecy rang out – 'Whatever you ask in my name I will give it to you. Ask, speak out your secret thoughts and desires. I want to give them to you now. Ask now, claim by faith and you shall receive.' It was more than a prompting to ask, rather a shove, and in quick response, Alan lifted his voice:

'Lord, give me an army of 10,000 in this area.' The people all rose up in faith praising God and claiming 10,000 with Alan. As a hush came across the meeting he sat down, thinking, 'What have I done?' Flooded with doubt and condemnation he poured out his heart to God. A clear young voice sounded above all the others as again God spoke to him in prophecy:

'Do not doubt and condemn yourself. Didn't I invite you to ask? As you have asked, so I will do.'

That evening became a landmark. God was going to give us 10,000 here in our district. We did not know if it meant one large church or many related ones. Our asking seemed so huge and unrealistic in the cold light of day, but we knew what God had said, we had heard his invitation to be audacious.

'I must learn to run a big church, we must organise ourselves for large numbers.' When Alan first said such things a clammy feeling settled in my stomach. 'Oh, Lord, don't let him lead the people astray.' I was slow to believe.

Yonggi Cho's name became a household word, 'The Fourth Dimension' was our bedtime reading. Leaning back on our padded headboard, we tried to visualise a church of 10,000. Our faith was stimulated. God is God, he is the same in England as in Korea. When Yonggi Cho reached out in faith for his first 10,000, it must have been in the realm of impossibilities even for him. Again and again we found ourselves talking about faith and impossibilities in the same breath.

Alan longed to see the Full Gospel Central Church, to see the living demonstration of his heart's desire. He knew that in Seoul he would meet those who could tell him how to build a large church. We prayed.

Around the world to Seoul

The phone rang, with a familiar voice on the other end. 'We've prayed about it for a couple of weeks, Alan. We think you and Eileen should go and visit Yonggi Cho's church. Get your tickets and we shall pay the bill.' We could hardly believe our ears, we were to go to Korea. Dates were fixed, tickets bought and extra food left in the freezer for our abandoned family. Everything was complete except for one important matter; we had no money. I mean money for hotels, travel and food whilst away. Strangely we hardly gave a thought to the problem. It was God who was sending us, it would be God who would take charge of the details.

Shortly, before we were due to leave, we went to The Downs Bible Week where Alan was part of the ministering team. We hitched up our caravan and joined another three thousand campers at Plumpton, some in caravans and others in tents. The site was arranged with church groups together, like a miniature camp of the Children of Israel in the wilderness. Alan stood on the high platform one night and looked out over the evening meeting. 'A good crowd, yes,' he thought, 'but this group is smaller than Dr Cho's home cell group leaders meeting! What must it be like to have a church of 10,000 each Sunday?'

Towards the end of the week a cheque was pressed into Alan's hand. 'Take this Alan, it's for all the extras you will need on your trip, and have a good holiday.' We thanked the Lord: when he sends, he always pays!

Our route was to take us via Thailand and Hong Kong to Korea, followed by a brief holiday in the States before returning home.

Land of the morning calm

'Land of the morning calm' was how the in-flight magazine described Korea. We had boarded the Korean Airline plane at Hong Kong along with a crowd of heavily laden Koreans returning from a shopping spree. Once we were seated I couldn't take my eyes off the air hostess. She looked as if she had walked out of one of those hand-painted Korean screens. Her features were so delicate and her skin like porcelain. She wore the traditional national dress, an elaborate full-length gown in silk with a long flowing bow attached to the bodice; then she spoke and bowed deeply. It was all so foreign. Although we had lived in India for years and travelled widely, somehow nothing I had seen before related to this young lady from the other side of the world.

The characteristic change in the note of the engine noise warned me that we had begun our descent to Seoul, the capital of Korea. Craning my neck I looked out of the window trying, like a greedy boy at a banquet, to take in the whole view at one gulp. There were the familiar paddy fields, a patchwork of different shades of green through to brown, some for a short moment glistening in the sun. Dotted here and there were random splashes of bright blue and red, the roofs of little houses. The city came into sight, cut in half by the wide meandering River Han. With a roar we taxied to a halt on the tarmac. Formalities soon finished, we walked out wondering which way to go.

All the signs and notices were written in Korean and no one seemed to speak any English. We made our way to the phone but didn't know which coin to put into the box. After a frustrating five minutes trying to decipher the instructions a young man asked in English if he could help. In no time at all he had dialled the number and we were talking to the reception desk at Central Church. Warmly we were welcomed. 'Yes do come straight to the World Mission Centre, we have a guest room prepared.'

We asked the young man who had come to our aid if he knew the church.

'Oh, yes, everybody knows Central Church. It's over the river at Yoido.'

He wasn't a Christian but interested and quite well informed about the Christians of Seoul. Kindly he put us into a cheap taxi – he was quite sure we wouldn't want the expensive tourist one. Leaning in the window he gave the driver careful instructions and waved us on our way.

We both felt incredibly excited. Here we were in Korea, driving through the streets of Seoul.

Our route from the airport took us past open-fronted shops like those of India, but the roads were a different story, all well constructed and wide with many lanes of fast moving traffic. Eagerly scanning the skyline, we counted the churches. They were everywhere, big ones built in western styles, at times as many as five in view at a glance. We feasted our eyes on the new sights as the long drive to the church took us through large residential and commercial areas. An old man wearing a tall black hat, baggy white trousers and shirt was riding an elongated bicycle like a stretched-out version of an old delivery bike. But most people were well dressed, in western-style clothes, as they wandered about on the pleasantly warm evening.

The taxi turned to cross the River Han. Seoul is a city that is still heaving itself out of the devastation of war, and the fine bridge, like all the roads, looked very new.

Now we were entering the government district. The pavements were wide and looked almost deserted (we later learned it was a public holiday) and then right in front of us was the most impressive domed building. I knew the church was large and I expected it would be grand but this went far beyond my wildest imaginings. Then as we drew nearer we saw that it was not the church but the National Assembly Building, the South Korean seat of government, and there, within a stone's throw, was the Full Gospel Central Church. Not quite so impressive as the National Assembly Building but magnificent in its own right. The tangible evidence of faith and perhaps, if the world really knew, the real seat of government.

The new republic

North and South Korea together form a stubby finger of land bounded by the Sea of Japan on the east and the Yellow Sea to the west. South Korea, a republic since 1948, occupies that half of the peninsula south of the Thirty-eighth Parallel. Its total size is just less than Scotland and

Wales together, much smaller than I had expected. Today's growing population of more than 37 million lives mainly in the coastal and urban areas.

In a hurry, trying to thread our way through the crowded pavements of Seoul, we realised a lot of people lived there; in fact seven million. The bus queues were usually long, but the service frequent. People are good-natured and polite. There is a kind of family atmosphere once on the bus, the elderly are given seats and the children shared around on laps. The 'survival of the fittest' mentality is often prevalent in huge cities which creates a ruthless desperation in powerful crowds. But Seoul was different. Although bustling and fast, it possessed a friendly quality.

North Korea, a communist country, is known as The Democratic People's Republic; they have no relationship with the South. Like divided Germany, Koreans suffer with many families torn apart by an ideological barrier. Instead of a wall dividing the two halves a so-called demilitarised zone runs from coast to coast, 155 miles long and about 3 miles wide. Only twenty-five miles North of Seoul are two, half million strong armies poised against each other. A demarcation line has been drawn, a ceasefire agreed, but the war has never ended.

Korea is a beautiful mountainous land with deeply indented coastlines and fine natural harbours of which Inchon in the west and Pusan on the east are the largest. The war stripped the land of trees but now, through a strenuous planting programme, the mountains are clothed. We walked up a hillside between adolescent saplings and clambered to the ridge where a line of huge oaks stood as sentinels. I wondered what stories they could tell. Somehow we think when we visit a country as far away as Korea that everything should be different, but not so; once in the countryside and feeling God's good creation, there is a sense of being at home. Grass is the same, good to smell, cool and delightful between the toes, or just to lie upon. Many of our garden weeds and wild flowers flourish in the undergrowth and stepping stones across a brook could be on a hillside anywhere in Britain on a perfect summer day.

Most of the minerals and industry were in North Korea, so since the cease-fire in 1953, South Korea has concentrated on the development of industry to complement its traditional farming way of life. As with so many other nations this has led to the movement of people from the land to the new cities and towns in search of work and bigger pay packets.

Wars and rumours of wars

For centuries Korea has been involved in a tug-of-war between Russia, China and Japan. Russia held sway between the years 1897–1905 until the Japanese went to war with the Russians. The armies trampled their way through Korea until Japan finally annexed Korea and reigned supreme until the end of the Second World War in 1945. For thirty-five years the Japanese treated the Koreans in the same fashion as the Babylonians had dealt with Judah. They carried away all the educated and skilled workmen. Utilising their traditional abilities the Japanese built for themselves new crafts and industries which flourished and helped to make Japan rich. The Emperor Hirohito of Japan considered himself to be divine. He made an edict that all Koreans should bow down and pay homage to his picture, as King Nebuchadnezzar gave command to the exiles in Babylon when he erected his golden image. The colonial Japanese systematically endeavoured to stamp out the Korean language and all their rich heritage of art and culture. Only Japanese was to be spoken. The rule was severely imposed with harsh penalties.

Japan treated Korea as its own back garden. Whatever crops grew were taken across the narrow sea to their masters' kitchens. As the paddy fields produced their harvest soldiers were waiting like vultures to carry it away, so that the Japanese could eat rice, the Koreans millet.

The young Yonggi Cho grew up during these years of cruel Japanese occupation.

The Second World War that had dragged on came to an abrupt halt as the atomic bomb flattened Hiroshima and humbled Japan. Its repercussions were immediately felt in

Korea. Hurriedly the Japanese left, defeated, the end of thirty-five years of occupation, but sadly not the end of warfare for Korea. The Russian army moved into the North. The Americans into the zone South of the Thirty-eighth Parallel. An uneasy truce prevailed for five years, time enough for the endless stream of refugees to put down their roots and try living again.

Then, one Sunday morning in June 1950, Chinese communists crossed the Thirty-eighth Parallel and started the war machine in motion all over again.

Seoul, an ancient city which existed one thousand years before Christ, at the time when we were in our Bronze Age and fighting off Celtic invaders, again shuddered under the impact of hostile armies. The population fled south; Seoul was reduced to a heap of rubble. Four times she was to change hands as the battle ebbed to and fro. Violent convulsions induced by war gripped the whole land. Tanks, army columns and exploding bombs had scattered the people. Hungry wandering groups of refugees were in search of food and safety.

In July 1953 the troops drew back again to the Thirty-eighth Parallel. Three years of horror had accomplished nothing except to make hundreds of thousands of women widows and children fatherless.

Slowly the reconstruction of South Korea started again. The bridges across the River Han in Seoul were rebuilt once more. With the fresh air of liberty in their lungs, Koreans rallied to resuscitate their nation. The worn remains of this ancient civilisation pulsed afresh as new life burst forth, filling not only the body but the heart of the nation too.

The first missionaries

The Christian history of Korea is very short – about one hundred and fifty years. Probably the first missionary to take the gospel to Korea was Dr C. Allen, an American Presbyterian who journeyed there in 1845. Some Roman Catholics established themselves at about a similar time, as it is recorded in the violent story of the Korean Church that two thousand Roman Catholic converts were martyred in 1866.

In the same eventful year an Englishman, Mr Robert Thomas, working for the Bible Society, landed from an American ship at Pyongyang. The hostile authorities resistant to foreign vessels pelted the ship with burning brands. The frantic crew fled for their lives, but were cornered and killed. Looking at the fearful chaos all around him, Brother Thomas must have almost despaired. He had endured so much and come so far to deliver his consignment of gospels. The moment called for quick decisions, a choice between burning with the ship, drowning in the sea or risking his life with the Koreans he could see on the land. Resolutely he waded up the beach carrying his precious load towards the murderous mob. Suddenly blows rained on him from every side. He was beheaded on the spot. It seemed that the soil of Korea was thirsty for martyrs' blood. Later fishermen found the blood-stained tracts and gospels floating in the shallow sea. They pasted them upon the walls of their homes. When resting, these literate fishermen would read the Word of God and before long the death of Robert Thomas bore fruit.

It was not until 1884 that Americans Underwood and Appenzeller settled in Korea and became her first resident protestant missionaries.

And the spirit came

Fifty years later in 1907 revival broke out in Pyongyang, now the capital of North Korea, and simultaneously in scattered places all round the world the Spirit fell. Miners in South Wales were dancing on the pews of tiny chapels; the hills of North India resounded with song as the Khasi tribe flocked into huge churches, repenting and praising God. News of the visitation at Asouza Street, out of which grew part of the pentecostal movement, prompted hungry Christians to search their bibles.[1] 'What is a pentecostal experience?' they asked themselves. Were these outpourings of the Spirit coincidences? No, it was God making a worldwide declaration of the countdown to the second coming of Jesus.

Today, derelict chapels with nail-scarred pews are the only evidence of what God did in Wales at the turn of the century but in Korea, a Church, growing at the rate of a million a year and out-stripping the population growth many times, speaks for itself.

When the Spirit fell upon the Christians in Pyongyang they were fired with a zeal to take the good news to the whole of Korea in one year. Not content to keep the blessing to themselves, like those lepers outside the gates of Samaria, they had to tell. Even though the Japanese-Russian War was in progress on Korean soil, these freshly empowered Christians evangelised the whole land. They raised the money, sent out missionaries and printed one million copies of Mark's gospel, selling seven hundred thousand in one year. Soon the country was dotted with groups of Christians. The powers of darkness were under attack. After five long centuries the ruling Yi Dynasty fell, toppled by the shock wave of God's Spirit through the land. Bondage to the old Confucianist heritage had gone. Our sovereign God was establishing his kingdom. At times the intense fire of the Spirit cooled, but its flames were never completely extinguished. The revival surged in waves.

The nationalistic fervour which swept the country in 1945 after the Japanese left provided the next new impetus to seek the Lord. Joyful Christians crowded the prayer meetings thanking God for their deliverance. Sadly in the north the heavy communist boot soon came to crush the fervent Church, and their freedom and joys were short-lived. But like plants that had been 'hardened off' before planting out these Christians were tough, their daily lives perpetually revolving around hard times. As persecution increased many escaped south, some went underground, and the blood of others was poured out: they joined the great company of martyrs.

Then in 1953 the whole story was repeated yet again; a fresh wave of persecution and a fresh wave of the Spirit.

Christians in the north faced the frightening reality that they were on the wrong side of the Thirty-eighth Parallel for freedom. What else could they do but pray. Thousands gathered even at four or five o'clock in the morning in the open air, and with one voice they stormed the heavens. When twelve thousand at once were on their knees, in the cold Korean winter, the communist authorities felt the challenge and all too soon moved in and took control. Faithful Christians were subjected to the most violent atrocities.

'Several Christians were crucified by the Chinese communists and hung on crosses for days until they died in torment. Faithful witnesses who did not cease from spreading the gospel of Jesus had their tongues cut out by the Red Chinese. Children caught in Sunday School were deafened; inhuman communists pushed chopsticks into their eardrums and so destroyed their sense of hearing.'[2]

Such barbaric acts prompted another stream of refugees to seek a way to the south. All roads were sealed, yet thousands escaped through mine-fields, past armed sentries hidden in transported goods or disguised. God blinded the eyes of the guards whilst his precious children made their way to safety. He had given his promise to be a father to the fatherless and a husband to the widow. He pities their plight. Countless women who did not know if their menfolk were alive or dead took their children and after committing themselves to God who was their only protection, walked out into the darkness with the hope of freedom pouring courage into their hearts. 'Please let my baby sleep,' must have been their cry.

Koreans echoed the words of Shadrach, Meshach and Abednego who said long ago, 'Our God whom we serve is able to deliver us from the burning fiery furnace', and so, they walked in the fire, crossing no man's land. I wonder if a fourth person walked with them whose appearance was like a son of the gods?[3]

Seoul received a great influx of Christians who had touched eternity and shared in the suffering of Christ. Their only comfort was the God of all comfort, their way of access: prayer. In winter or summer and even in rain, they came in their thousands at four o'clock in the morning to pour out their hearts in unison, 'Oh, God, save our Korea and set the people free.'

The vigorous young church of Korea grows up from foundations soaked in martyrs' blood with walls bathed in prayer and washed in tears.

The church today

The vast throng waiting to go into the seven a.m. service at Central Church, viewed from our window, had not come to do their religious duty. Never! It was Sunday; they had come to worship God. He was life to them, their only reason to live. Like the slave who never wished to leave his master's house, there were old women who had made their gallant escape years back, now ready to serve their God forever. Younger people who were perhaps small babies bound to their mothers' back at the time of her flight, now bound in devotion to Jesus, filed up the steps into the church.

When we joined them, inching our way forward in the waiting line, I didn't for some reason feel part of the crowd. Rubbing shoulders with me were men and women who had a strong collective sense of purpose, almost as if they knew something that I did not. I was a spectator, not a participator.

The atmosphere made a profound impression upon me. Here was a whole community caught up in the fire of revival; their hearts were ignited with a flame that warmed and filled me with wonder. I prayed that a spark of that fire would be lit in my own heart before we left for home.

More than 15,000 people flooding into the services seven times each Sunday makes Central Church the busiest place in Seoul and probably in the whole of Korea. 10,000 can be seated at a time in the uniquely designed main building, shaped like a modern Albert Hall with graceful flying balconies all round.

A young man showed us to one of these balconies, where earphones were provided for foreign translations of the service. Once the people were seated the gangways, foyers and even the steps outside were covered by people sitting on the floor. Whole families found any nook or cranny to squeeze themselves into. The gymnasium, a large building alongside, takes another three thousand overflow, and is linked to the main meeting by closed-circuit television.

We sat staring at the close-packed congregation. A sea of people. Standing on a raised podium was Dr Cho with two other men, one of whom I recognised as Dr John Hurston who has been with Dr Cho in the work from the beginning.

The service was formal, strictly following the order on a printed sheet given to each of us as we entered. They sang translations of Western hymns to adapted Western tunes. They recited the Apostles' Creed and the Lord's Prayer. A full orchestra sat on a raised area; alongside was a gowned choir which led the singing and rendered an anthem. Although compared with our way of worshipping it appeared traditional, it wasn't dull. I noted in my diary that day: 'the service ran to a strict timetable – it seemed closely structured but throbbed with life.'

The efficiency of the organisation was impressive. There was always someone on hand to help, whether to show us to our seat or to adjust the headphones. The smoothness with which the mammoth task of gathering the offering was accomplished left us speechless. Without any feeling of hurry the bags were passed round the whole congregation in a shorter time than it takes in many a smaller church. The full bags were all collected together by deacons and deaconesses who carried them in a long procession to the front. That morning Dr Jashil Choi, the mother-in-law of Dr Yonggi Cho, received the offering and then led the congregation in most fervent prayer. There was nothing formal about this, the people raised their voices in supplication. The translator explained to the foreigners that the offering that morning was for missionary work in Japan and Dr Choi was pleading with God to save the Japanese.

Koreans have been thoroughly converted. Those who

once hated their captors now pray for them, those once robbed of their goods and money now give freely to see the church established in Japan.

After Dr Cho had completed his sermon, a simple word of exhortation of how to overcome and prevent depression, he gave an invitation to all who did not know the Lord. Powerfully in a few words he encouraged the people to trust God for deliverance, healing and salvation. Immediately all over the auditorium men and women stood in their places. No soft lights and gentle music or endless persuasive words, just firm decisions being made in the cold light of day. Amazed, I saw well over one hundred people quietly stand to their feet. One man openly weeping although there had not been a shred of emotion in the meeting.

Despite myself I felt plenty of emotion. Surely it was God – the one who quietly compelled response from so many.

As quickly as the people responded to the invitation, deacons and ushers were by their sides. Women went to the women and men to the men. After words of counsel and prayer they were handed a small packet of helpful literature and, most important, a card upon which they were to give their name and address. That information is passed on to their nearest home cell leader who will visit the person until there is a clear commitment.

Dr Cho prayed for all those who had responded. Ardently the congregation joined their prayers with his and called down blessings.

We smiled as the notices were translated for us:

'Pick up all your belongings – do not leave anything behind – if you do you will never see it again!' And he meant it! Carefully we obeyed and slipped into the current of people shuffling their way out into the sunshine.

Our first day in Seoul was packed with surprises and we were like children gazing into a kaleidoscope, every fresh look fascinating. The departing congregation made their way to waiting buses and taxis with the aid of church traffic controllers. These men wear distinctive yellow armbands as they shepherd the people onto the public transport and control the traffic. If there was a medal to be awarded for outstanding crowd control, undoubtedly they deserve it. The bus queues are hundreds of feet long but the transport system apparently copes, with the aid of a fleet of chartered buses.

We stepped into the lift to return to our room and were accompanied all the way up by choruses over a loudspeaker system. New impressions had come at us so thick and fast we needed time for them to sink in.

We were beginning to realise that the Full Gospel Church is an organisation of such diverse magnitude that its operation is more akin to governing a fair sized town than pastoring a church in our terms.

We looked forward to discovering a little of how it was done.

TWO

Meet Dr Cho

'I would like to speak to Dr Cho's secretary,' I said hesitantly.

I wasn't sure if the uniformed man at the desk had understood. Rummaging in my file I pulled out a copy of my letter to Dr Cho.

'Look,' I said pointing.

Quickly he scanned it and said in broken English, 'See Dr Cho?'

I didn't feel that I qualified for that honour without an appointment, but before I could say anything more, the receptionist directed me to Room 208, Dr Cho's office.

I went up the stairs and scanned the doors on the second floor.

'Shall I knock at 207 to enquire if I'm really allowed to go into 208?' I asked myself. Before I could make a move someone opened the door from the inside, where I could see a small waiting room and office. Introductions were soon made and before I could explain why I had come Pastor Lee Huan Kyou shook my hand and greeted me as an honoured guest.

'We've been expecting you, I'm so sorry you didn't receive my letter. This morning we prayed for you,' he said encouragingly. Turning to another gentleman he introduced me and explained that I had come to write a book about their church.

'Yes,' he said, 'we see your coming like the visit of the Queen of Sheba – everything is open for you to view!'

With more encouraging words Pastor Lee put me at ease whilst kindly waiting to escort me to meet Dr Cho. I was soon to learn that Pastor Lee excelled in the ministry of encouragement.

To a Western mind Korean names can be quite puzzling. Sometimes Dr Cho's name is written Cho Yonggi, back to front in our thinking. Traditionally in Korea the family name comes first followed by the given names. When Koreans and others who follow this pattern travel in the West it causes some confusion, so slowly the habit is changing. Even the name of the president of Korea, on occasions appears in Western form in local papers. For convenience Dr Paul Yonggi Cho now writes his family name last and has added the christian name Paul. A bible name is acceptable, easy to say and international.

I began to peel off my layers of winter clothing. My first visit to Korea had been in summer, but January presented a very different view of life. The bright sunshine was deceptive, it was ten degrees below zero and outside the biting wind had stung my face.

Time passed with many comings and goings: a smiling couple stepped out from the inner office; efficient kindly-looking men in business suits hovered about waiting their turn. Casual clothes were nowhere in evidence, perhaps symbolic of their serving attitude. One by one they disappeared inside, with nobody remaining very long. An older lady with a most serene face went through the door. She was slightly bowed, the modest bow of Korean courtesy seeming to have become her fixed posture. Pastor Lee said, 'That's his mother-in-law.' At close quarters she looked so different to the mighty woman I had seen on my first visit to Korea, when she led the vast congregation in prayer.

Room 208

Dr Cho walked to greet me, his arm outstretched, and with a firm brotherly shake he smiled and welcomed me to sit. The comfortable seats were arranged in an open rectangular shape. Dr Cho sat in a large leather armchair with Pastor Lee and myself either side. Very conscious that I was there without an appointment and that he was an extremely busy man, I put the bare bones of my mission before him.

'The Lord has led me to write a book about your church and the mighty work God has done. To get the facts straight I need your help. I want to be able to write the truth and stimulate faith in the western world that what God has done here he can do in our countries. This church is unique, but I'm convinced it is significant to the whole world.'

He sat very still listening without relaxing back in the chair. Hardly a flicker of movement crossed his face as he gave me his full attention. Perhaps my English accent was difficult to follow. In his neat suit he looked like an efficient business man. His whole manner and personality spoke order and strength. I knew I was with a truly great man.

Kindly enthusiastic he assured me of his co-operation and that of his staff, and added that a room had been prepared for my stay.

For some time Dr Cho spoke in Korean to Pastor Lee instructing him, as I was later told, to take care of me and for all arrangements and visits during my stay. We all stood, and as I left he wished me well with oriental formality. Dr Cho's next appointment was a radio programme and Pastor Lee hurried away to send a telex for Dr Cho's visit to Manilla in the Phillipines.

No superman

In the pulpit Cho is the most relaxed happy preacher. He exhorts the people with a huge smile and wide flung arms. He chats to the multitude as if to a few in a family circle. The warmth of his personality, his love for the people, and genuine humility comes across. Frequently he exposes his own failings and readily asks for prayer. Certainly he doesn't create a superman image for himself. Where possible Pastor Cho is among his people. He has his critics and some are none too Christian in their attacks. Recently his healing ministry came under fire in the local newspapers. Turning to the congregation he said, 'I feel it, pray for me.'

When invited to speak at Seoul Women's Aglow Dinner,

laughing and happily relaxed he shared his testimony. Exposing the painful dealings of God in his life he used his own shortcomings to illustrate God's ways with his people. He never hides behind his success. He is not a man with a front, but genuine and urbane.

The ideal wife

Dr Cho's wife, Grace Sunghai Cho, is a most accomplished woman with a lengthy list of achievements to her name. Besides sponsoring a children's orchestra and composing tunes for the choruses her husband writes, she is a skilled pianist with a Master's Degree and a Professor of Music at Horso College. I visited Grace Cho in the busy office of the Youngsan Publishing Company where type-setting machines clicked and telephones rang. It was obvious that her position there as executive director was no honorary title. 'Yongsan' means spiritual mountain. The publishing company is part of the church's activities, the fruit of Grace Cho's vision.

There is a dignity about Grace, a very modest woman, most reluctant to talk about herself. Someone said to me that there was something special about her. She was like the first lady about there! I wondered what part she had played in the development of the largest church in the world. No doubt she had paid a price. Her husband refers to her as a 'faithful help in the ministry'. She, more than anyone else, must have agonised with him during their years of trial in the buildings of this great work.

There was a period, after the decision was made to construct the present church, when funds ran out and the building ceased for eight months. Depression settled upon the work and discouragement whittled down the congregation. A blanket of frustration and despair enveloped Cho. At that time Grace was pregnant but she found strength in God to stand with her husband, although wounded in heart seeing him so low and not so easy to live with.

Huge sums of money were needed so like many others in the church they sold their flat, which only recently had been fully paid for. They had enjoyed its security for so short a while. Its price went to the building fund as a seed of faith. They moved into a part-constructed church apartment. Many months of trial followed. With her first baby on the way Grace earned their living from music tuition, because Cho declined any salary till the financial crisis passed.

Yes, surely she shared the cost of building the work. Only a wife fully knows the strain which brings her man to breaking point and to even contemplate suicide. Every fibre of her being feels it first for herself, then for him, and then again in frustration, because she can't do anything to take it away.

I asked her how often in a month her husband was at home.

'Probably about seven to ten days, but it varies,' she said.

They have three sons, aged eleven, twelve and sixteen. She went on to say, 'I don't want my sons to know only their mother: they need their father when he is home. I push them towards him and they ask him questions, so that he can understand them. These days I don't want to know all the concerns of my husband but we talk and discuss many things. Sometimes I give him suggestions which if it seems right he will take, or a thought he may preach. Of course we always pray and read the scriptures together.'

An incredible strength pervaded her whole demeanour. She had tapped deep wells of grace. She didn't just exist in a rather trying situation but was fulfilled and secure. I asked her if she had always felt that way. She smiled.

'Once it was hard with my husband away every week Monday to Friday before the children were born, but I sought grace from God. Then he gave me so much work to do that now I'm busy and satisfied.'

Grace is an extraordinarily peaceful and loving person. As soon as she started to talk about her husband her face lit up. She shared with me how God had led her to publish his sermons in book form.

'I was in a conference in the United States praying about the many invitations my husband received from all around the world. He could never go to all these places, so why not print his sermons in books? They could travel anywhere. When I shared my vision with my husband he encouraged me, so we have now published 195 books in Korean and six titles in English. I think we have published in nine different languages.'

The secretary chipped in. 'No, it's sixteen now.' Grace continued, 'Next to the bible, I think my husband's books are the most important!' We laughed. Grace is a great admirer of Dr Paul Yonggi Cho.

The family have a flat on Yoido Island, near to the church, where Grace besides all her other activities is a loving wife and good mother. You may wonder how she manages so much without neglecting her responsibilities at home. In most eastern lands it is easy to find household help and a member of the church faithfully serves her, so thankfully Grace Cho can leave her home in trustworthy hands. Strangely the professional woman in the east is far more likely to continue in a successful career after marriage than her western counterpart.

Yonggi Cho's priorities

Pastor Cho's life must be phenomenally busy and Grace Cho's is not much different. They are two astonishingly able people who have found grace to bear their load with ease.

One would think that such a high powered way of living would cause strains and tensions in their relationship, but this is not so. Dr Cho is a true pastor to his family. Early in their lives difficulties did arise as they can do in any new marriage, especially when there is tension between being with the wife and serving the Lord. A zealous young man can quickly dismiss his wife's needs as unspiritual demands, till he has revelation about God's standards in marriage. When Jashil Choi asked her son-in-law if he liked living with his wife he was shocked at the challenge. His eastern thinking coloured his attitudes. He provided for her: she had good food, nice clothes, a house and he didn't beat her; what else did she want? After all a wife is there to serve her husband whether he is kind or cruel; she is not expected to complain.

His zeal for the Lord was strongly mixed with personal ambition, a driving mongrel passion to see God's work established and himself a success. How we wriggle when this powerful emotion is touched; how many marriages and families have been sacrificed upon its altar. The young Yonggi Cho fought with the problem in his heart: 'This is unreasonable; how can I meet her demands for love and fellowship? How can I make her feel appreciated?'

He thought about it for a long time and became convinced it was the devil trying to turn him from his chosen path. His dear wife became very withdrawn, she felt so neglected by Cho's continual absence from home.

He could stand it no longer. If forced, he was even prepared to make a choice between his love for his ministry and that of his wife. He was driven to praying in desperation: 'Lord change her or otherwise we must separate!'

Through this experience God taught Yonggi Cho how to order his priorities. The hard lessons learnt in those early years of his ministry have been reaped bountifully in successive years not only in his own home life but also in establishing secure relationships in the homes of his very hard working staff. Many times in ministry he repeats the exhortation he so faithfully obeyed:

'Your first priority is to God, to love him with all your heart, and your next is to yourself.'

To many of us that sounds quite shocking, but Jesus said, 'Love your neighbour as yourself.' In that light perhaps we do not give ourselves a sufficiently high priority. The Lord showed Cho how essential he was in his purposes and in order to fulfil all his calling he must give himself the luxury of a regular satisfying spiritual diet, constantly living in the fresh reality of the presence of the Holy Spirit.

His third priority was his wife and when he had children they would be the fourth. Patiently the Lord explained to Yonggi Cho how fundamental are marriage relationships.

What testimony would he have if his wife were to leave him and he ended up divorced? He was to love her as Christ loved the church, to give her fellowship and make her secure. His fifth priority, after the family, was the church, a complete reversal of thinking.

Whatever the Lord says to Yonggi Cho he does with all his heart, his obedience is complete. Out came his diary and many evangelistic campaigns were cancelled. God said to him, 'Give every Monday to your wife,' and so began a new lifestyle. 'Whatever you want to do today, honey, we'll do.'

More than being a dutiful husband he was obeying the Lord and it wasn't all that easy; in fact at times he was utterly frustrated. They visited the shops till his feet ached, idled in the park on fine days, or perhaps had a meal out. Half the time he was gently boiling inside thinking of all the things he could be doing. However, practising tender loving words with a splash of appreciation spiced their life and soon transformed his wife, and the painful lessons learnt were never forsaken. Even today with the enormous demands upon his time, Monday is the day off for himself and all the staff.

Schooldays

Outside a gang of muffled rosy-faced small boys yell and shove each other in an impromptu game of chase on the low walls about the newly constructed sixteen floor World Mission Building. Life wasn't so carefree for the young Yonggi Cho, growing up in a village near to Pusan during the hard days of Japanese occupation. With wartime deprivations, life was one long hard struggle for his parents. They had five sons and four daughters, Yonggi Cho being the first son.

Finding enough food to eat and hiding it from the filching hands of the Japanese fully occupied his mother. In a secret hiding hole at the back of their home lay what precious grain they could reserve from their harvest.

In winter the Korean climate can be very cruel with weeks of sub-zero temperatures, so warm clothing had to be made and the busy fingers of his mother and sisters were never idle. Living in an atmosphere of continual siege where any possession could be robbed by the local army forced the family, like others, to create ingenious ways of existing with the ruthless authorities. Underneath, hatred and bitterness grew in their hearts.

The position of teacher in Korea was highly respected. Therefore the Japanese reacted by removing all Korean school teachers from office. No Korean could have an honourable position, they were the lowest of creatures in Japanese eyes. Each day from the age of six years, Yonggi coaxed along by his nine year old sister, walked the mountain path to his local school to be taught by a Japanese soldier. Korean children are so winsome and beautiful, with round chubby faces, but even their appearance never softened their soldier-teacher. He was the conqueror, they were the vanquished. Daily the children were exposed to cruelty and outright torture. Besides physical abuse young Yonggi was subjected to mental bombardment. The children from their youngest days were brainwashed to think and act Japanese; Japan not only occupied the land but attempted to annihilate the culture. The people were only permitted to speak Japanese, have Japanese names and follow the cultural habits of Japan, honouring their Shinto gods and the emperor. This foreign mode of conduct was harshly enforced in the classroom, where the non-conformers were cruelly beaten. Any apparent disrespect to the emperor, the Shinto gods or Japan brought fury upon the children. Once Yonggi Cho's stomach was jumped upon until he was boggle-eyed and gasping for breath. Cruelty, even to young children, knew no bounds.

Life's a miracle

The Korean eldest son holds an immensely important position in his family. He traditionally inherits the privilege and responsibility of perpetuating certain religious activities. It becomes his duty to offer sacrifices at his ancestors' tomb; and eventually to raise up a son in his place to continue the age long custom. After his father dies the eldest son becomes the head of the house and even his own mother would respectfully obey him.

Growing up as someone special certainly had benefits for Yonggi Cho as he enjoyed extra attention from his parents and respect from his brothers and sisters. He was elder brother. You can imagine their anguish when Yonggi, now in his teens, was ill again. It appeared no one could help. For a number of years Yonggi's health had vacillated. His loving mother had nursed him back from near death more than once but now his condition seemed hopeless. The doctors pronounced him incurable, both lungs riddled with tuberculosis. He was beyond the reach of drugs or medical assistance, even if the family could have afforded it.

'You have about three months to live, young man,' the doctor pronounced.

Yonggi Cho, eighteen years old and constantly vomiting blood, was now too weak to leave his bed; continual coughing racked his emaciated body. The comfortless days offered no consolation. Almost everyone seemed to be a refugee. The war was ended, but peace hadn't come to impoverished families.

His father struggled yet again to find food enough to feed their many mouths. The winter was cold. Korean houses are normally warmed by an under-floor heating system, but there was no money for fuel that bitter winter. Yonggi, burning with fever, shivered with only a thin blanket.

Youthful ambition pent-up, almost too weak to ask why, he lay powerless and frustrated. Only three months from hell, except God chose to step into his life, overturning cultural traditions on the way.

A young high school girl knocked at his door. Without an invitation she walked into his room, sat down, read the scriptures, prayed and talked of Jesus. What audacity! Yonggi was furious. What was a girl doing coming uninvited to a man's room? Openly rude, he swore at her, 'Get out and take your religion with you.' The Christian dog didn't know how to behave, yet she persisted day after day, reading, singing and believing. He despised her. After five or six days Yonggi Cho found himself actually anticipating her visit; he lay waiting for the knock. There had never been much conversation between them, and when she eventually came she sat quietly, strangely impervious to Yonggi's hostility her face a picture of peace. That day he noticed her face and wondered how she could persist when he had been so angry with her.

'Why?' he asked. 'Why are you are coming here?'

Tears rolled out of her eyes which touched Yonggi's heart. She told him of her Jesus who could heal and transform him. Down on her knees next to the sick man she showed him her bible assuring him the answer was there.

'You haven't time to read from the beginning, you will be dead before you finish. Begin here.'

She opened at Matthew's gospel, encouraged him to persevere and left. She never returned again.

As he read he met Jesus. He was the one who gave life, healed everyone who came to him. Hope grew in his heart, perhaps he didn't have to die. He took a deep breath and instead of coughing and gasping a warm glow settled on his throat and chest. 'If I'm dying it feels good,' he thought, and fell asleep. When he woke he had an urge to get up and walk a litttle. Day by day he grew stronger. He was healed and he knew Jesus.

Recently a teacher in Seoul was telling her class of nine year olds the thrilling testimony of Yonggi Cho. One little girl who had listened intently said, 'A high school girl! How hard that must have been for her and she had so much work and studying to do. She was only a girl, how could she speak to a Buddhist young man.' The concept was almost unbelievable.

Yonggi Cho doesn't even know the name of the young lady. She faithfully brought the Word of God to him, then disappeared. Never could she have imagined what God was eventually going to do through that desperately sick young man. When we witness, who knows whether we could be speaking to another future Yonggi Cho.

Emerging into life

Once strength began to return to his feeble body he made his way back to the hospital. The X-ray showed perfect lungs with no trace of the violent infection remaining. A miracle had snatched him back from death.

Old ambitions surged around inside. With a healthy body what could stop him now from qualifying as a doctor? All his energies were flung into work and study; he was going to succeed. The doctors respected his diligence. He was a good student, obviously intelligent. But God had other plans. To Yonggi's horror two years later the old symptoms of tuberculosis returned; he was again coughing up blood and gasping for life. Success had come almost within his grasp only to slip away. His sick body could not take the last few steps. Unable to continue with the pace of life he left the hospital thinking rest would improve his health.

All the while he was studying English, till he was finally capable of interpreting the message preached by Pastor Lou Richards, a missionary at the Pusan mission. Before long he was freshly aware of why God had given him life. He was to serve the Lord, not make money or a name for himself or even satisfy his own desires. He belonged to the Lord, but he still had T.B. 'What do you want me to do with my life Lord?' he prayed. He set apart a day to ask God about his future and healing. Late that night, when he had almost given up, God came into the room. Eye to eye he spoke to him.

'Every kingdom of the world will crumble and fail. You are very ambitious: preach and establish my kingdom which will never crumble.'

In the awesome presence of God, the Spirit came upon him and he found himself praying and praising in an unknown language, then fell deeply asleep.

When he awoke it was almost like a dream; but no, it had been reality. That encounter set the course for his whole life. In the clear light of morning his worldly ambitions lay dead and buried. The way opened for him to go to the bible school where he slowly regained his health. No doubt the unconverted Yonggi Cho was a stubborn strong willed individual but circumstances hadn't created those traits, he was just born that way. Whatever the challenge once he had got the bit between his teeth he was determined to go and succeed. If he had remained healthy he would have followed his chosen course in life and most probably have become a distinguished medical doctor.

Life is woven from various kinds of experience, some significant, others traumatic, a few delightful but most mundane. Although Yonggi Cho's childhood and youth was a patchwork of all of these during times of hardship, danger, warfare and extreme poverty lived in the darkness of Buddhism, none of those experiences have made him what he is now. The most important event in his whole life was the time he met Jesus. What he is today is what God can do with a man. He can take a physical wreck and give him life, he can take a spiritual wreck and make him a channel of spiritual power. Yonggi Cho's life owes nothing to the past. He is an altogether new man revolutionised by the mighty power of the Spirit. Yonggi Cho says, 'God makes the pastor – the pastor makes the church!' But how does God make the pastor? I looked into Yonggi Cho's background to discover the secret. An outstanding leader of indomitable character, full of faith; what was God's method for bringing forth such a man? A crucible, in a fire; not a comfortable place. The strength of the wild horse must be tamed.

The Lord allowed sickness to be the rein upon Yonggi Cho's early life. All his pent up desires and plans were continually frustrated by his feeble body not keeping up with his driving spirit.

Beginning in ministry

At last free from T.B. and enjoying good health he had thrown every ounce of his energy into establishing the church. Now his frustration was not with a sick body but with other people. As the work grew so did his tension; his mongrel passion was being exposed. Working day and night he spent himself, but the burden was too much. Mentally he was cracking and the pain in his chest was almost continuous. Something had grown in Yonggi Cho's heart which caused everything to become an intolerable burden. That something was pride.

At twenty-seven years old, inwardly, Yonggi Cho was puffed up with arrogance. 'Of course', he says, 'I didn't let it show on the outside.' At times he was seething, wanting to send his co-pastor, John Hurston, away because he had become a burden to him; also his mother-in-law, if only he could persuade her to go as a missionary somewhere! He was convinced he was the one with the Word of God and the people could only be blessed through him. He says that the people all worshipped Jesus through Cho. Suddenly the Lord yanked the neck of his wild horse.

One day there were 300 to be baptised and Cho had already preached three times. For the previous few days he had been feeling weak and permanently tired but he drove himself, thinking, 'I must baptise them. How else can the people be blessed?' John standing by watching, saw that after the effort of immersing 150 Cho was blue and trembling. 'Shall I take over?' John offered. Unbroken and stubborn Yonggi Cho refused and continued, exhausted, at the end he could hardly pull himself from the pool.

Although physically almost finished, his mind was racing on. That afternoon an American evangelist was expected to arrive, and Cho determined to meet him. Refusing all offers of help, foregoing his food, he dashed to the airport, met his guest, checked him into a hotel and rushed back again to translate for the evening service. He was ready to collapse, spurred on only by sheer stubborn willpower laced with self-seeking.

The preacher was the energetic physical type, jumping all over the platform. Not to be out done, Yonggi Cho not only translated but acted the part. The anointing of God had left him so with greater effort he tried vainly to fabricate a blessing, raising his voice.

A searing pain went through his heart, he fell to the

floor gasping for breath. He felt his heart flutter and stop. 'John, I'm dying,' he gasped. Drifting into unconsciousness, he complained secretly in his heart. 'Lord, if you have to chastise me couldn't you do it privately in my office!'

He was carried out on a stretcher and taken to the hospital. But how could he stay there? The doctors knew he had quite a reputation as a divine healer. What would they think? He demanded to be taken home to his apartment and refused any medical attention. His patient deacons took him home.

The following week was misery. Yonggi Cho says, 'I felt I was on a never ending elevator going up and down. I could hear shrieking devils, God seemed a million miles away.' He seriously thought God had given him up and he was on his way to hell. Day after day he cried out to God to forgive his arrogance and pride. He confessed all his sins to John then again to Jashil Choi and his deacons. He repented and said, 'I will never be arrogant again.' Yet he had no comfort or relief.

Sunday came, the 'dedicated' Cho was determined to preach. He refused to give John his pulpit. Pale and weak he went to the platform and lasted for just eight minutes before collapsing. The faithful deacons carried him out but a few hours later at the second service, he insisted that he should preach again. This time he stood for only five minutes, hanging on to the pulpit, and anxiously they gathered him up and again carried him out. The church was in uproar. He had reached rock bottom. One of his deacons, a famous doctor, examined him. 'Pastor you must give up your ministry. Your heart is so bad you will be dead if you continue.'

Lessons at rock bottom

But how could he give up the ministry to which he knew God had called him. Groping his way back to God he began to read the scriptures and pray. There were so many questions but no answers. God didn't seem to be listening. Then about three weeks later the Holy Spirit came to him as he lay on the floor crying, writhing and vomiting. 'Cho, I am going to destroy your kingdom and delegate your ministry to others.' Perplexed, Cho thought the church wanted only him. 'You are dispensable' the Holy Spirit said. 'I will build my church on my word.'

Continuously Yonggi Cho was confessing his sin, struggling in his spirit, longing to be right with God. Daily he pleaded, 'Please Lord, please heal me,' yet no answer came. Till one day God said, 'It will take ten years for you to be healed.'

'Ten years! Oh God!'

'Yes, for ten years you will live in this suspense and pain.'

And it was ten years Cho suffered, never knowing if he would live or die. If he preached, the fear of collapsing always stalked him. There was not a shred of security left in his life. Again and again he would say to his new wife, 'I shall be gone any moment.' He felt as if he was dying all the time. His heart was greatly enlarged and a further heart attack could have taken him at any moment. He suffered what is commonly called nervous and mental exhaustion. He was worn out. In his testimony Yonggi Cho says, 'You know, God destroys you if you have arrogance and self-pride. I know, I tasted it for ten years. I was completely destroyed. Then I started to say to God, "Survive or not, live or die, prosperous or pauper, I don't care, I want to become yours." That death experience completely destroyed me.'

The wild horse needed a strong active body that would not weary when fully expressing all his driving desires, so the Lord touched his body. God knows how to harness the power of an indomitable will and to rein in vagrant energy and transform it into submitted strength. In time, the wild horse became the lowly donkey lifting up Jesus.

Troubled, perplexing times followed as Cho endeavoured to find ways of continuing his ministry with a body that could hardly cope with staying alive.

With a new humility he sought God in prayer and in the scriptures. 'Lord I don't understand what you mean.

I want to obey you but how am I to delegate my ministry to others?' God gave him light and opened his eyes to fresh truth. When he lacked the physical strength to actively pastor his church which had now grown to two to three thousand God stepped in and began to show him how to establish the cell system; the church in the home, which is now the foundation of pastoral care and evanglism in the church.

God makes the pastor. Yonggi Cho has been 'well made' in the relentless loving hands of God. The man who once had aspirations which flew higher than being 'just a pastor' now has the world's largest congregation where, as he says seriously, 'God is the senior pastor and I'm his assistant.'

His staff love him; he has the ability to draw from them the very best. Pastor Hyan Kyou Lee said, 'My whole desire is to serve God; I do it through Pastor Cho. I serve and thank God all day long praying to be completely devoted to him, that through Pastor Cho and Full Gospel Central Church I might serve the Father faithfully.' The breaking and making experience through which God steered Cho has made him into a true leader, head and shoulders above everyone else, out ahead in vision, godly character and faith.

Faith to give away

'Cho is an expert at making the impossible possible' said one of his pastors. It is that amazing gift of faith which works so powerfully through Pastor Yonggi Cho that more than anything else has produced a church in Seoul which is now among many other things, a tourist attraction. It has become a phenomenon. He has faith to spare; it infects all those who come near him. Meeting by meeting his congregation is envisioned and revitalised. Faith pours into their hearts to think big, to think success not failure, and to possess what God has promised. Like all faith it began as a small mustard seed and has gone through many painful stages of development. Today Full Gospel Central Church is the substance of things hoped for, the tangible evidence of faith. The mustard seed has grown into a huge tree.

Who could have believed that such a dream could have come true when in its humble early beginnings the church met in a leaking tent in a Seoul suburb in 1957. Yonggi Cho said, 'The Holy Spirit began his first church with three thousand on the day of Pentecost so I never set my sights any lower. Even though there were only five people in my first meeting my heart was set upon three thousand.'

In his own inimitable way Yonggi Cho constantly refers to visions and dreams and incubation. What does he mean? His visions and dreams are squarely rooted in the Word of God. 'From Genesis to Revelation, all is yours' he says, 'read and saturate yourself in God's Word and see what he shows you, and what you see you can have.' In this way he encourages the people to enter into the promises and vast possibilities open to those who simply believe. Abraham looked to the east and to the west; as far as he could see, all was his; yet he also had to possess. Following Abraham's example, Cho encourages his people, there is a further stage to be walked by the person who will actually possess what he sees. Yonggi Cho carefully divides between believing and seeing in your mind, and possessing in your spirit. He explains, 'Get the vision and hold it in your heart by dreams and imagination. Don't let the sight of what God has shown you slip away into the mists of unreality. Keep dreaming of how it will be when God unfolds his purpose for you, bring that dream constantly into light and reality through prayer and the fresh application of the Word of God. That which you have seen must be born in you, filling all your concern in the same way as a mother who is pregnant with a child.' He calls this stage incubation, being pregnant with a dream. Just as a pregnant woman's life is bound up with her burden, just as she knows no freedom till the birth, so it is with 'incubation'. The burden is born in you; if it is possible for you to forsake it or cast it aside then no conception has taken place, it is still only a hope.

Faith is like mountain climbing, there is always a fresh peak to attain. Spurred on by the sight no training seems too tough for climbers. They want to make the top, even though it means hardship, disappointment and exhaustion on the way before the triumphant flag is raised at the summit.

Through impossibilities strewn upon the way of faith our own fragile resources are exposed but the man of faith glories in his weakness, knowing that it is God's opportunity to display his power. Like mountain climbing every fresh victory only whets the appetite and stirs the desire to try again. A man who climbs Everest begins his training programme on the small hills near home. Yonggi Cho's first attainments of faith were: a desk; a chair; and a bicycle. But today the same principles of faith are applied to win millions of souls.

Do past victories in faith help when confronted with a new challenge? Yes, surely a rich confidence in the heart says, 'God can do it again,' but with every fresh experience of faith there always comes the crisis point. You have heard God, believed and know what he is going to do, yet you wait, and wait. You must hold on at that point of crisis, continue to believe and wait. Many who begin never possess because when they reach that crucial time they run out of strength, as if they had pushed a heavy lorry almost to the top of the hill but just can't take it over the brow.

Many wonder how to differentiate between presumption and faith. It is difficult because the division is between flesh and spirit and outwardly it is not always easy to judge. The surest safeguard against presumption for those who desire to obtain faith goals is a humble and meek walk with the person of the Holy Spirit. The man who desires, even secretly, to build something for himself has opened the door to the subtle temptation of presumption and he himself can then be so blind that he does not know what has happened. Finally, the proof of genuine faith is in actual possession.

Faith is highly infectious. As I joined the throng of people surging up the steps into the main auditorium I could feel the expectancy that was in their hearts. They had come to pray, believe and possess. All about them was the tangible evidence of the possession of faith; they knew prayer worked. They knew believing God was not in vain. They knew the impossibilities of this life were very possible with their God.

Dr Cho ministers with an air of bold confidence, encouraging and assuring the people that God is as good as his Word. The gift of faith flows through Yonggi Cho as a dynamic ministry. He is able to share his vision of faith in such a way with the people that they are quickened to stand with him, to believe, work and possess. Pastor Cho, as they call him, 'knows God, and knows what he is going to do. We can trust his words and move on with him in faith.'

Standing on the podium in the middle of his vast congregation, Yonggi Cho with his hands in his pockets said, 'Some say I am greedy.' Then he laughed, and pointing to the people he said, 'You get a holy greed for souls.'

THREE

The biggest church in the world

It is hard to believe when walking around the Full Gospel Central Church complex that it had very humble beginnings.

During bible school days, Yonggi Cho and Jashil Choi teamed up for various evangelistic projects. She recognised in him a young man who had the hand of God upon his life and prayed faithfully for him. Eventually when they simultaneously graduated in 1958 Sister Choi started evangelistic meetings in a slum and Yonggi Cho, healthy again, full of the unbridled zeal of youth joined her as the preacher. Their grand opening was under a makeshift shelter of a tattered ex-army tent with only five people present, including Sister Choi's daughter and an old woman who fell asleep!

All around them were squalor, poverty, sickness and hunger. These were desperate people, but although Cho knew he had the answer in Jesus to every one of their needs they didn't come.

From the outset the work was bathed in prayer, they were both mighty pray-ers. Unlike rational westerners who readily look for fresh methods and techniques these simple servants of God got on their knees, and now, with renewed vigour, fasted and prayed, till God heard them. Miracles began to happen and significant healings took place that made the whole district talk. The word spread rapidly and now the people came running. Powerfully Jesus moved among them meeting them where they were, in their needs. Cho could preach with conviction that Jesus is alive, and before their eyes was the evidence as God manifested himself in power. The work grew and it was then that Dr John Hurston, a seasoned American missionary, joined them.

Things hoped for

Even while preaching to a mere handful of impoverished people, Yonggi Cho had his eye on 3,000. He preached as if they were sitting there; he talked of a large congregation, dreamed and prayed about it till some thought he exaggerated or lived in unreality; but he knew the secret of Mark 11:24. 'Therefore I tell you, whatever you ask in prayer, believe that you have received it, and it will be yours' (Literal translation).

By 1961 in three short years the church topped 1,500. John Hurston and Yonggi Cho collaborated to raise money for another building. All the while Cho talked, lived, expected and behaved as if 3,000 were a fact.

Growth continued at a pace; Cho had no notion where the people were coming from. The cells had been established and were following a healthy natural pattern, dividing and subdividing so that within five years an extension on the new building was necessary.

The man who sought success for himself was daily dying, yet fruitfulness flourished to the glory of Jesus. To him people were not like production targets, goals to be attained. Driven by genuine heartbroken compassion for those going to hell, the whole church, leadership included, spent extended times in prayer and fasting. Natural growth continued as they shared the heart of Jesus for the lost.

Yonggi Cho makes light of the ten years of suffering he endured. Despite his inability to deal with the everyday affairs of his church, it continued to grow and grow. By 1969, only eleven years on from its small unlikely beginning, 8,000 members rejoiced at the ground-breaking ceremony on Yoido Island for the new church building, which is in use today.

To see the construction work through, three million dollars were needed. There followed a terrible financial crisis when Cho beat himself with many recriminations.

He didn't doubt his guidance to build the large auditorium but he had added an apartment block at the back. Had all this catastrophe occurred because he was trying to do it his way? Swept over by feelings of disillusionment, despair and even thoughts of suicide, Yonggi Cho held on. A faithful group gathered on the concrete foundation to praise and rejoice. They believed God would vindicate their faith. The whole church sacrificed. Dr and Mrs Cho sold up their home and like many others gave the proceeds to the construction work. People gave their time and energy, even labouring on the building site, others sacrificed things that we would consider necessities of life, like money for their children's education. In the upheaval, the biggest heart-tearing for Yonggi Cho was to see his congregation scattered. But it was not for long. Only four years later, 10,000 people crammed the building, rejoicing and praising God, and the following year the membership doubled. Faith was vindicated, but at a price.

Today the church is the largest in the world and you may well ask why Yonggi Cho didn't establish hundreds, or even thousands of smaller ones? A big church which expresses the bigness of our God and the power of his salvation has always filled Yonggi Cho's vision. He says that if you aim to produce a large church, automatically many smaller ones will be produced in the process, and dozens of such churches have been established. Both he and John Hurston are mighty advocates of the large church. Its very size has an impact of power and is a visible evidence of the success of the gospel. To be a witness in the company of thousands of others encourages boldness even in the most timid Christian. Obviously with a large church facilities can be available for every area of spiritual need and expression. There is scope for so much more that is satisfying without resorting to para-church activities. A large church which only provides a large audience for one man's ministry is a disaster as a church. Full Gospel Central Church is a living organism with ministry and life in every member. Strangely, despite its vast size, almost too hard to comprehend, there is a sense of amazing unity in the whole church. The people belong to cell groups and various organisations in which a genuine family feeling prevails. They express a wonderful sense of identification in a strong bond of loyalty and affinity to their church, and travel long distances to be there amongst the whole family for a Sunday meeting and perhaps even once or twice during the week.

The depth of loyalty that exists in the hearts of all the underleaders, whether they be pastors, deacons or cell group leaders, is a major factor in holding the church together as one body functioning in peace and unity.

The loyalty expressed to Dr Cho as a person and to the church is profound. Dr Cho has never endeavoured to hold the whole work to himself. On the contrary, he has been willing to send men out, encourage them, and even support some to establish other works, by which means a number of satellite churches have been built.

A functioning pyramid

The majority of us are intrigued as to how a church of such gross proportions can function in any way like a church. After all it is as big as two or three fair-sized towns put together. But unlike a town, where people live and make their own lives, in the church every individual from granny down to the newest babe, is known and cared for. Each one is someone's responsibility.

You may wonder whether in a church so large, there is any love, sympathy or concern for the individual, or if it is just a vast empire of some efficient businesslike tycoon, impersonal and cold. Quite the contrary. Despite its huge size, there is the same feel of relationship, love and concern that one would experience in a small fellowship. Surprising? No, not really, because these are genuine Christians with a sincere love for God and each other. They are bound together in a common purpose of establishing the kingdom of God.

I secretly feared that if I scratched below the surface of this vast organisation I might be horribly disappointed and find it shallow. I didn't need to fear. The closer I got to the ordinary individual involved in the day to day running of the church, the closer I got to genuine godliness and simple Christ-like virtues. These are people of sincere faith.

Many get nervous when we talk about a pyramid-type structure. The question is immediately asked, 'And who sits at the top of the pyramid?' Well, Yonggi Cho sits at the top of this pyramid and he humbly says, 'I am the under-shepherd, but he who rules this church is the great shepherd of the sheep. I seek to do his will.' The pyramid in Full Gospel Central Church gives one the feeling of plenty of space and fresh air. There is room to move, to express one's feelings and personality. Personal initiative is not regarded as a trait of rebellion but an attribute of zeal. It is pounced upon and used to its fullest measure. Enthusiasm and zeal are considered most valuable.

The organisation of Full Gospel Central Church is flexible, capable of continuous extension, without weakening the structure or upsetting the whole by every necessary change. John Hurston says, 'We grieve the Holy Spirit by not organising the church efficiently.' He likens the structure to the electricity system in a building. All the power we need comes to the box outside, but what we actually do with it depends upon the wiring we have established inside. In many churches the only wiring ends up in one outlet, the pulpit, but in Full Gospel Central Church a network of outlets has been laid with the continuous possibility of further extensions. Providing an organisation through which the Spirit can efficiently flow is the responsibility of leadership: if you want to boil a kettle, provide a socket! If you want a functioning church provide the structure through which the Spirit can flow.

It is impossible for an observer to grasp fully the extent of all the activities and functions in Central Church. A living organism is in a state of constant change and adaptation, so it is hard to keep abreast. If a need becomes evident it is provided for. Many of the activities stem from prayer and vision within the departments of the church. For example 'Love Line' is a telephone counselling ministry, which sprang out of concern by the Koinonia University Graduates' Ministries. They now have their own office with telephone lines which are open twenty-four hours a day manned by trained housewives, students and others. The church's ministry and organisations are as diverse as to meet the needs both of young girls working in 'sweat shops' and of millionaire businessmen: from bible studies with taxi-drivers to the Logos fellowship, formed for the puprose of uniting the intellectual talents of 103 faculty members of various universities who are in the church.

Men and women's fellowships

Some of the most dedicated serving activities flow out of these two fellowships. Without their sacrificial deaconing work each Sunday, the meetings would grind to a halt. At about six a.m. on a Sunday morning, the buses begin to arrive from all over Seoul. These are chartered by the various housegroups to bring their people in to the meetings. The men's fellowship are there from that early hour to organise the parking and guide the people to their seats. This is a massive undertaking – like controlling a football crowd seven times a day, except that it is better disciplined.

As the people pour out of the buses, half running, they pass street vendors with Christian tapes blaring music from transistors and an enterprising beggar collecting a small fortune from the sympathetic passers-by.

Together the men and women's fellowship provide ushers for all the meetings. The women are quite a feature of the life of Full Gospel Central Church, always in the beautiful Korean national dress. Traditionally in Korea no woman would have the prominence of greeting guests and showing them to their seats but Yonggi Cho has persisted in replacing national traditions by bible culture. Women are emancipated by the gospel to be respected and given a rightful place in the home and church.

Another activity of the women's work is the preparation for the communion. The vast communion service is once a month, and it follows days of vigorous activity to provide the bread and wine, which are home made. Thousands of communion cups have to be washed and filled. Can you imagine the task?

Sunday the day of rest!

At present the services in the main auditorium begin at seven o'clock then nine, eleven, one, three, five and lastly at seven in the evening. Dr Cho ministers on four occasions, snatching a light lunch in his comfortable room between meetings. Provision is made for the many foreign visitors, with a Japanese translation in one balcony and English in another.

Month by month the number of over-flow halls is increased. The newly opened World Mission Building is now in use with 2,500 people on each of the first few floors. Underneath the church is the long low-ceilinged Canaan chapel where thousands more meet, not to mention the gymnasium, the Antioch, Bethlehem and Jerusalem chapels all crowded with people shoulder to shoulder watching small T.V. screens. At the feet of Yonggi Cho on the platform in the main church is a line of small monitoring T.V. screens so that he can see those in each of the overflow halls. At a point in each service he turns and specially greets them. Even though they don't get into the main meeting they come week by week.

As well as finding overflow halls for the adult meetings, Sunday School and young people have to be provided for. Many of the offices are invaded by large classes and small groups. Eager youngsters huddle up for a bible study sitting on mats squeezed in anywhere they can, even under the stairs or outside in the sunshine, ignoring the cold. Their teachers are mainly young people who are well trained, baptised in the Holy Spirit and a joy to behold.

In March of 1981 it was estimated there were over 7,000 children in the Sunday School. But over and above that number, in the whole of Seoul, 46,000 are involved in children's cell groups, which meet on a weekly basis led by dedicated volunteer trained workers. Most of these children are unconverted, brought in by friends. They so enjoy their meetings that given half a chance these enthusiastic youngsters would meet each evening if possible.

Programmed to grow

What is the secret for the phenomenal church growth, and how has it been maintained so consistently year after year? Cho casually says, 'Anyone can have a large church if they will follow the growth principles I teach.' I would not want you to get the impression that it is only following a set of principles that produces growth. Again and again his workers would look in vain when asked for a reason for the gigantic size of their church. They would shake their heads and say, 'It's just God.' True, it is God, but God found in Yonggi Cho a servant whom he could use. The following principles Dr Cho presents as his essentials for church growth. This is how I have analysed them after visits and from his preaching, tapes, teaching and writings. They are not listed in any order of importance.

1. Leadership and goals
2. Home cells and a functioning body
3. Trustworthy competent pastoral staff
4. Prayer and fasting
5. A flexible and efficient organisation
6. An outgoing missionary commitment
7. Faith
8. The Holy Spirit

These principles are worked out in every area of life in the church so I have described them in the manner I saw them functioning. Cho is not teaching theory. His church growth principles are not academic but the fruit of twenty-five years of experience and success. He is qualified above all others to advise on church growth.

1. *Leadership and goals*

Most important is God's man – equipped and hard working. If his church is going to grow the leader must have an attitude and desire for growth. It is here that the majority fail. So often we have settled for smallness, that which we feel capable of managing or what seems average. When measuring success our comparison can only be with others of small desire and achievement. We have all grown up in a climate where it would be extreme to expect 3,000 as a basic minimum, as they experienced on the day of Pentecost. The devil has sold the church a huge lie till we have come to accept small congregations as a norm; some even prefer them thinking they better serve the purposes of God. But Jesus died for the whole world; his heart wants to draw everyone in. If we are ever going to see growth it will be through leadership with the same unrestricted heart to the world.

After an attitude and desire for growth there must be a plan for growth, which is worked out in realistic goals. A leadership which does not present specific goals before the people will never succeed in growth. Where there is no goal, there is no motivation or ability to measure achievement or failure. Growth requires God-given realistic goals which are spelt out to the people, not in vague terms, but broken down into attainable responsibilities for each one. This is a prime task of leadership. The pastor must regularly present challenging goals before his people which provoke, stimulate faith and give direction and purpose to the whole church. Then it is through the cell group system that they are realised.

2. *Cell groups and a functioning body*

It was in 1964 at the onset of Cho's ten years of trial that the home cell groups were first established. Those painful years were a unique training experience out of which evolved God's pattern for church growth. His illness kept him so weak physically that he was forced to implement home cells and use the ordinary church members to lead them.

God told him to delegate his ministry, which puzzled him, leading him to search the scriptures looking for understanding. Then by revelation the Lord began to speak.

a. *The Pastor makes the church* The good advice Moses received from his father-in-law, Jethro, shed light for

Yonggi Cho on how to shepherd his multitude. 'Choose able men from all the people, such as fear God, men who are trustworthy and who hate a bribe; and place such men over the people as rulers of thousands, of hundreds, of fifties, and of tens. If you do this, and God so commands you, then you will be able to endure, and all this people also will go to their place in peace' (Ex. 18:21,23).

He wondered how it would work, because the people still wanted to come to him. Avidly he read his bible, and in Romans and Acts every page seemed to say, 'the church in the house', 'the church in the house'. What did this mean? His concepts of ministry only recognised trained professionals, but what was this? Ordinary people earning a secular living, not specially trained or even Christians of long standing, pastoring the church in their homes? What was more, it seemed that Paul also recognised churches in the homes of women. A revolution had begun in Cho's thinking.

Quite unable to care actively for his ever growing flock he thanked God for light. Somehow he was to create churches in the homes and delegate his authority to other leaders. First he spoke to his deacons, explaining to them his dilemma. God had called him to serve, he knew he was in the ministry by God's ordaining, but physically he was incapable of fulfilling his calling. Most of his days were spent resting in bed or reading at his desk; to visit his people was impossible. With great care he presented his plan to the deacons.

'I would like to divide the people into groups of which each of you can be responsible. You can pray for the sick, teach the people, evangelise and preach. I will give you my power so that you can do this ministry,' he explained.

Where we would say 'delegate our authority' he says 'give my power' which exposes the heart of delegation. His deacons were being invited to take up a ministry on behalf of Cho, doing it in his place, which he would endorse before the people. He gave up the power for that ministry to them, so that they could function freely under God but under Cho at the same time. It was an opportunity for each of them to flourish in new gifts and enjoy the power of God flowing through their lives. Unfortunately these beautiful blessings were denied them at that time because they failed to break out of their traditional strait-jackets. Cho wasn't prepared for the negative reaction that followed.

'Pastor, that's what we pay you for. If you can't do it we will find another man who can. We are not trained for this; besides we have our own responsibilities!'

Greatly discouraged Cho again turned to the Lord.

'Use the women' the Lord said, but Cho was scared. He could imagine all kinds of catastrophes. It will break up the marriages; Korean women aren't like Americans, they naturally stay in the background.

Then followed an amazing conversation with the Holy Spirit.

'From whom was Jesus born?'

'Mary, a woman,' answered Yonggi Cho.

'On whose lap was he nurtured?'

'A woman's.'

'Who took care of him through his growing years?'

'A woman.'

'Who went with him and supplied all his earthly needs throughout his ministry?'

'Women.'

'Who came first on the resurrection morning?'

'Women.'

'Who first met the resurrected Jesus?'

'A woman.'

'Whom did he command to tell of the news of his resurrection?'

'A woman.'

'Women nurtured and cared for the body of Jesus when he was on earth; today they will do the same for his body, the church. Men will never surround his body and supply its needs, but women will.'

Almost fearfully Pastor Cho called the women and explained to them his vision for the church. With sympathy and concern they listened and understood the predicament.

They were godly, with a desire to serve but felt themselves quite incapable of meeting the needs. They longed to help but how could they? They were useless, only untrained women.

He encouraged them, 'With the power of the Holy Spirit you can work; you go under my authority.' Painstakingly he encouraged them, building up their desperately low self image. Finally persuaded they promised their help and he commissioned and sent them out to form cell groups. The city was divided into sections and in each place a woman was put in charge. She was given responsibility to care for all the pastoral needs, to pray for the sick, visit and preach. Although the women felt so inadequate they were prepared to serve their pastor in that fashion for God's glory.

Soon the church was in uproar! Dissensions and troubles abounded: some mothers had neglected their children; family quarrels were breaking up the homes, some women became arrogant and neglected their husbands, others were teaching their own ideas, even heresy! The men were so angry, Pastor Cho didn't know which way to turn.

Back he went to God, 'Father, I've only done what you told me to do, what's wrong?' He encouraged himself in the Lord. His natural reaction was to scrap the whole plan but the Lord restrained him and said, 'Once the Holy Spirit is flowing through a properly ordered structure all will be well.'

So he carefully set about rectifying his mistakes. As he looked more closely he could see that not all was catastrophe. A few mature women were ministering with great success. Taking them to one side and leaving the others he showed them how they were to be bearers of his message. The women were only to teach what he instructed, not their own revelations, so he specially taught them and in this way regulated how they functioned. He gave certain commandments. The women were never to lay hands upon the men and to prevent rivalry among the people who were very poor, the women leaders were instructed not to take more than tea when visiting. Giving lavish food to visitors is part of Korean courtesy and no one wished to be outdone, but some were far too poor to compete.

These simple instructions brought order and the cells began to grow. Again and again Cho divided them until he was burdened with the demand of so many cell leaders bringing reports and needing instructions he appointed associates, one over each thirty cells. But before long there were too many associates bringing him their problems so then he appointed ordained pastors to be in charge of the associates. Thus he evolved a pyramid type organisation which has proved capable of continuous expansion.

The cell groups come under the pastoral care department of the church and today are divided into twelve large districts which are sub-divided into sections.

The district head is an ordained pastor with direct responsibility for the section heads who are mainly women with a pastoral responsibility for well over a thousand people. Each section is broken down into cells of eight to fifteen people. Every four or five cells elects a representative who liaises with the section head. It is through this simple structure that life and teaching flows and growth goals are realised.

In most of our churches talent and godly ability lie dormant. Without encouragement and direction, even the most gifted will achieve nothing but in Central Church everyone is put to work. The growth goals for the church are shared with the pastors, section heads and home cell leaders.

b. *Cells with a goal* The cell leader is motivated by the responsibility of attaining the goal laid upon him so he gathers his group of eight to fifteen people and envisions them. Motivated by a sense of responsibility to achieve their goals the home cell seek God. The goal directs the people, unifies the group and draws out their individual strengths to obtain their objective. Together they can discuss, pray and work. Success is shared in the joy of souls saved, and failure is also shared in prayer and fasting.

Full Gospel Central Church grows by each cell adding

to itself and dividing as necessary. Pastor Cho gives a yearly commission for growth to all his cell leaders and then, by all means, motivates them to be successful in their work. He says, 'If you ask someone to climb a mountain without showing them the top, will they climb? I clearly show the way, then, with a little enticement, persuasion, recognition and appreciation of their excellent work, giving them privileges in the church, and even using slight intimidation because of the fear of the Lord, I send them out. My people work and in 1981, they brought in 100,000 new believers. Every month I check my cell leaders for progress. I encourage and admonish them. They are my most trusted workers.'

The cell group system is the means of motivating every believer within the church. Evangelism and pastoral care are not left to a few paid church employees, but the whole body is caring and expressing the love of Jesus. It is the opportunity for every believer to serve the Lord. It brings satisfaction, fulfilment and growth. Instead of being Sunday attenders, people are co-workers with their pastor and their God. Everybody is utilised; man or woman, young person, even the children. Each has got a part to play. Truly this is a priesthood of all believers. No one is debarred from ministry. Everyone with the life of Jesus has the opportunity to share.

Every week 300,000 copies of a four-page newspaper are produced, sufficient for everyone in the congregation to have their own copy as well as distributing it to schools, colleges, army and navy bases and to any one who is interested. In it everyone can read the pastor's message, various new items, and most important the bible study outline for the home cell meetings held all over the city. This printed guide is used by all the groups and avidly followed by pastors in other churches. (One young pastor preached Cho's message week by week in his own congregation till one Sunday he was dismayed when he failed to get his copy of the paper!) Each cell member is encouraged to go through the outline and come prepared to the group. The leader has a fuller guide from which she teaches the set bible passage which is also expounded at a central Wednesday meeting for those who can attend. Every meeting has prayer and bible study.

c. *Winning their neighbours* How does a cell set about winning someone for the Lord? The group gathers and has a brain-storming session. Who they ask, in their locality or amongst their acquaintances has a problem? They have been taught to look for those in need and then meet that need through the sufficiency they have in Christ. Sickness, problems and heartaches are their opportunity. Rather than running from them they look for them. Once a contact is identified, collectively they pray and the appropriate person will visit. It is pointless to bombard someone with the gospel who perhaps is desperate concerning a loved one who needs healing. So rather than preaching the gospel the group prays and encourages the family to believe that Jesus can heal. For instance when a woman's three-year old grand-daughter fell from the eighth floor, the Christian neighbour rushed to pray for the child. As they lifted her up she was whole. The entire family believed. They had seen a miracle.

On another occasion a Mrs Lee had been befriended and invited to the cell group meeting when the district leader was visiting. He ministered the word and afterwards, Mrs Lee crying said, 'That message was just for me.' She pleaded for the leader to come to her house and pray. Although the pastors make from seven to fourteen visits a day he laid aside other responsibilities and went. He found she had already received the Lord and the Spirit prompted him to lay his hands upon her. Immediately she was baptised in the Holy Spirit and began to speak in tongues. Afterwards she came regularly to the services, all night prayer meetings and prayer retreats.

Another story is told of Mrs Chou San Lee who had a neighbour who was demon possessed. She longed to see the man delivered and the family saved. So she fasted and prayed for three days. The neighbour was immediately released and the whole family brought to the Lord.

The people are vigorous, fearless witnesses to what Jesus has done for them. The strength of their own personal testimony has a clear ring of truth in the hearts of unbelievers. Their transformed, ordered, prosperous lives speak powerfully. Buddhist neighbours can see that the Christian's God is real and that he blesses his people.

d. *The web of love* John Hurston calls the cell groups a web of love around the city. They meet wherever there are people, not all in homes. Some are in factories, even on taxi stands where drivers meet for rest periods, still others are in hospitals, schools and colleges. The majority of the cells are amongst women and they meet during the daytime. Young people's and children's groups meet on Saturdays with men's meetings on Friday nights or Saturdays, as they can fit them in. However because of the long working hours most of the men are not able to participate.

The cell group system is the principle reason for Full Gospel Central Church holding together as a unified body. The cells are like the net holding the great catch of fish, 'Although there were so many, the net was not torn' (John 21:11) At present there are 15,000 cell groups, ninety per cent of which are for women and are led by women. Yonggi Cho said when interviewed in Britain in 1981, 'I was really discouraged on coming to the western culture and finding that they are no longer using women very much. In Korea, and especially in the Orient, women have been treated like donkeys or cows or mere chattels. Then Christianity came and right away set the women free and lifted the position of women so much that they are fully accepted as human beings in the church; when God calls them, they freely minister to the people. On one condition, of course – that they are under the authority of their husbands and the male pastors. So if the pastors are men and the husbands will give all the authority to them, the women have full freedom of speech.

'We are tapping the enormous resources of women in the church. I have 250 associate pastors, sixty per cent of whom are women. The women are helping to build the body of Christ. When I come to the western culture, sadly I find that all the women are kept silent in the church. They are immobile. They are such a fantastic resource, and so I feel sick in my heart. If the church of Jesus Christ developed them, then they would be a source of great blessing to the church.'[1]

3. *Trustworthy competent pastoral staff*

'Why don't you take 10,000 of the people and have a church of your own?' Cho offered one of his leaders, but none will go from him even with such inducement. They trust his leadership and are secure and fulfilled. The quality of Cho's efficient pastoral staff ensures continual growth. Any one of them is a mighty man of God in his own right with responsibility for thousands of believers. Quality is the hallmark of all their leadership.

Cho's mighty ten I was assigned to go with Pastor Yong Nak Choi who heads the eighth section of the seventeen which together make District Number One. He has responsibility for seventy-two home cells totalling 1,023 people. This humble man of God is 'just' a section leader.

Through thirteen cell representatives he efficiently pastors his seventy-two cells. Pastor Choi was typical of the self-effacing leaders in every department. In him was no striving for recognition or desire to make a kingdom for himself. Truly these men and women are of the same heart as David's mighty men, who came like an army of God to present all their gifts and abilities to King David. They were of a single mind to make David King.[2]

I visited a children's meeting where two to three hundred eager five year olds were crammed on to long pews with hardly a breathing space between. Out in front was a fine group of capable young leaders, not just controlling the crowd but impressively leading the children into the presence of God.

There was nothing amateur in the way things were done. Each leader had the children's full attention. The young woman who told the story could have been a professional actress, she played the part so well that a sea of little faces was held in rapt attention, watching her every movement, listening intently and responding vigorously when their turn came. It was the same with the song leader and the girl who led in prayer. She captured the little children's hearts and vision and led them to the Lord.

Good leadership can be expected in the principle areas of any church's life but there, even down among the littlest members, I found only the best.

The pastors all lead very busy lives, beginning at eight forty a.m. when the buses arrive at the church bringing them from all over the city. First they gather for a staff meeting led by the head of the pastoral department, or on occasions by Yonggi Cho himself. Each district office arranges its programme for the day, everything is well bathed in prayer and then the pastors in charge of the various sections get back into the buses to begin their day. Before they return they will visit new converts, contacts, hospitals, take meetings and do a hundred and one other activities which heaped together mean pastoral caring.

An emergency call came from a senior deaconess to visit Kim Jee Whan who lives in Dok San Dong, Seoul. For three years Jee Whan had been suffering from cancer of the liver and had not moved from his bed for eight months. He was dying and not expected to last the day. The pastor and the family gathered to worship the Lord as they waited for the sick man to slip into the presence of God. They sang and prayed, glorying in the Lord, but he didn't die. It began to get late but the pastor couldn't leave the family in such uncertainty, so he thought, 'Why not ask the Lord to heal him so that I can go home!'

They gathered round the dying man and began to pray and before long he regained consciousness, was alert and healed.

Within a few weeks his strength returned and today he is a walking miracle.

Testimonies of the powerful intervention of God abound; miracles seem to be part of the everyday happenings in the pastors' lives.

The pastoral staff, financially supported by the church, is augmented by thousands of lay leaders, deacons and deaconesses, the majority of whom serve as voluntary workers. Many women are occupied in a full-time pastoral capacity in this way with their husbands' support. It is people of quality like these who have imbibed the vision and faith of Pastor Yonggi Cho who are largely responsible for the church's growth. He never ceases to sing their praises and publicly honour them.

A large portion of Cho's ministry is stimulating and caring for his pastoral staff. He ministers the word to them so that they share his vision and heart. He pours his faith into them so that it becomes theirs.

Through this their loyalty is of the same stamp as David's mighty men. Cho's men and women stand about him like a trained army. Trusted, tried and proven they are a dominant fighting force to overthrow the powers of darkness and establish the King of Kings in his Kingdom. His leaders are like the cedars of Lebanon, ordinary stout wood, but as they have been incorporated into God's building he has overlaid them with fine gold. God is subduing the land before them because they have set their hearts to seek God and faithfully serve him.

4. *Prayer and fasting*

Praying for growth is no new idea. We all believe that a praying church is a growing church and without prayer we will never grow no matter how many other things we may have right. Out of all the principles that Cho lays down for growth, this one at least has been attempted by everyone who has longed to see souls saved. Feeling helpless we have been driven to prayer; in fact at times there has been nothing else we could do, and yet our prayers have produced so little. These lean years have taught us how to encourage ourselves. We have learned persistence and patience in prayer, waiting for God to step in and do something supernatural. Despite the set-backs and disappointments which most of us have experienced when praying we come up with no other answer. Our eyes are upon the Lord.

God answers prayer Praise God, in many places there is the beginning of a breakthrough as people see the fruit of their patience and persistence. We shouldn't be discouraged even though as yet we have not seen results to compare with the church in Seoul because if we are patient we will reap, especially when our praying is linked with God-directed activity.

The prayers at Full Gospel Central Church are marked by a certain characteristic. First of all they are direct and specific. Requests are made for particular blessing, situations and individuals. No one prays generalities. The prayers they bring to God are definite requests laid on their hearts by the Holy Spirit. Most often these burdens will be presented by the leadership when goals are shared together. They then become the incentive to seek God, hear from Him and take responsibility in prayer to see the issue through. The prayers are positive and where action is required, such as a kindness, a helping hand or a word of testimony, quickly the pray-er co-operates with God and in one sense brings the answer to his own prayers.

Many companies of believers although faithful in prayer do not necessarily grow. This especially happens when the prayer life of the church is mainly directed to personal holiness and turned in upon itself. That kind of praying never produces expansion. If our desire is for growth we must come to God with the definite request.

A great expansive love has grown in the hearts of the believers in Central Church. They cry and long for the lost. For them the burden of loved ones going to hell is intolerable. This quality of praying appears to purify the whole character, as an abundance of love flows out, surely this is true holiness.

The church that prays for growth will automatically find itself involved in evangelistic activity. The ability to evangelise is latent in so many unfulfilled Christians and praying for the harvest will act like a magnet drawing them out so that their ministry is identified. The determination to grow in Central Church is further expressed by those who fast as well as pray. The pray-ers share the burden which Jesus carries for the lost and are genuinely heart-broken about the plight of neighbours, friends and family who do not know Jesus. They fast because they are prepared to do anything to see them saved. Fasting with prayer is their expression of determination and total commitment to see the Kingdom of God expand and Jesus glorified by fruitfulness.

5. *A flexible structure and efficient organisation*

Growth means continuous change. Continuous change can mean continual upheaval. Growth that produces upheaval in the end will be counter-productive. The expansion at Full Gospel Church is so rapid, like cells growing in an incubator, that at any meeting probably half of those present would be new converts. The church is a continuously changing scene, with new faces being added week by week. How, in such a situation, can the people be provided with a sense of security? This basic need is built into the structure of the church through the house group system, where the people are gathered together in small caring units. Growth would surely come to an end if a factory atmosphere existed rather than that of a family. Any church which is looking for multiplication that brings them into the thousands, certainly requires organisation capable of providing security and a sense of belonging for the people.

Growth is not just people being added, but the church becoming mature. Central Church provides for the teaching of their new converts through bible correspondence courses and special classes as well as the home cell system.

There is no reason why any believer should fail to grow; everything is provided through the different departments of the church. The organisation of Full Gospel Central Church is itself continuously growing. This could be a hazard to efficient communication, but the system seems to work remarkably well. The whole structure is so simple, creating a flow from newest believer through to his section leader and right to the top. Everybody feels that they can be heard, nowhere do they come up against a wall of organisation or bureacracy. The heart of the church has grown and grown with a delightful feeling of warmth and love flowing through its very efficient workings.

Throughout the organisation there is a line of authority and accountability. This is not a strangulation upon the work, neither is it coldly legalistic, but beautifully counter-balanced by giving responsibility and freedom for personal initiative. The organisation of the church does not exist for itself, nor is it efficient for efficiency's sake. All the patterns of working have evolved with one purpose in mind – to see the church grow and Jesus glorified. Everything is submitted to this.

Dividing and sub-dividing does not occur only in the cell groups but also in every area of the work. As any unit becomes too large for efficient function it divides. The organisation is living, flexible and able easily to accommodate new departments and activities without disrupting the entire structure. It is self-propagating, producing its own additional leadership as required. The organisation is the servant of growth, built for change, and finds within itself the ability to adapt to every new need. There can't be any sleeping partners in the Church, its success depends upon the mobilisation of every believer and the functioning of every gift that God has given.

The activities of the church are so wide ranging that humanly speaking it would appear impossible for them to dovetail together, and yet through the line of responsibility and accountability each department is eventually answerable to the board of trustees who are the elders of the church. Pastor Lee assured me that Dr Cho is constantly aware of all that is happening, a feat made possible through the excellent structure that has evolved.

Growth will cease if it overloads the organisation, paralysis will then set in. The commonest symptom of an inefficient structure is over-worked leaders. Like the rest of us, Yonggi Cho has only twenty-four hours in his day. He has successfully expanded his twenty-four by utilising the time belonging to other men. This is genuine delegation, without which any work can only grow as big as the man and his ability in the twenty-four hours that are his. Through delegation, the ability to use the time and gifts of others made available through the simple structure of the church, Cho has proved to be a master at expanding his day. Most pastors would find about 300 people more than enough for them to handle. So far Cho has not reached his limit. The secret is delegation, the sharing of power.

6. *An outgoing missionary commitment*

The world is their parish Full Gospel Central Church has a zeal for foreign missions; the world is their parish. Yonggi Cho is firmly of the opinion that no church can grow unless it has a missionary vision. The attitude of heart that wants to see the whole world saved cannot fail to produce growth at home. Giving money to foreign missions as well as sending people involves the church in the missionary heart of our Lord Jesus. His desire for growth is worldwide and he delights to bless his children when he finds those who will share his vision.

The missionary programme of Central Church is not an activity of a few individuals but the expression of the whole church intent on seeing the gospel taken to the ends of the earth. They have a passion to see Jesus reigning worldwide in all the nations. Rarely a meeting goes by without them giving and joining their voices together in prayer for the spread of the gospel all round the world.

When the present church at Yoido was being built, Yonggi Cho made a pledge with God that if he would give him the ability to complete that huge construction he would then make foreign evangelisation a priority. The vast sum of money required to complete the beautiful building at Yoido was provided and the promise has been kept. We are commanded, 'Go into all the world and preach the gospel to the whole creation'. (Mark 16:15). Yonggi Cho considers this an important injunction laid upon the whole church and steadfastly he encourages his church to obey. Evangelism at home is not sufficient, the command is 'into all the world'. Full Gospel Central Church is certainly successful in extensively evangelising at home and bringing in thousands of souls, but that alone would bring little satisfaction to the heart of Yonggi Cho. The whole world calls to him.

As well as keeping the church alert to the needs of the lost, the missionary zeal in the Korean church is also an expression of gratitude to those who first came at great cost to bring the gospel to them. The foreign mission programme in Central Church is given high priority and Yonggi Cho counsels others, 'Whether your church is large or small obedience to the command to go into all the world is a foundation which must be laid. Missions are a priority. Each church should give a proportion of its income to the evangelisation of foreign countries as well as sending personnel. It is never a question of whether we can afford it; in fact no church can afford not to support a foreign mission programme.'

To neglect it is to starve the church of life, faith and growth. As the people get involved in missions where they give and go, the Lord will endorse their activity by causing the church at home to grow and even flourish financially; a sure way of preventing financial famine in a time of economic drought. Missionary concern turns the focal centre of prayer and desire away from ourselves and towards others. Life and maturity develop as people labour to send the gospel to places where they themselves will not reap the immediate benefit. Outreach is the very life blood of the church, or as Yonggo Cho says, 'a basic secret to church growth'.

7. *Faith*

Half a million by faith Dr Cho can't help but transmit his abounding faith through everything that he ministers. It appears to run off him; he even looks confident and full of faith. The bible says, 'Without faith it is impossible to please God',[3] and certainly without faith it is impossible to grow. Faith has been put to work in Central Church, and is directed towards definite growth. He has taught his faith and shared it so thoroughly that the people have imbibed his attitude to growth, so that even the most outstanding goals that he presents do not daunt them. They share his faith that they can obtain and they can grow. Cho says, 'There is no stopping faith. If I do not continue to thrust forward to possess more and more through faith, we shall slip back and stagnate.' So he continuously presents new visions of faith for his people. The present goal of half a million in 1984 is not left as a vague hope that perhaps might happen, but is a target for which he works and prepares. Already plans are made to cater for the doubling of the congregation in two years.

Where are they going to sit? How are they going to be accommodated? Who is going to transport half a million people to and from church each Sunday without bringing Seoul to a halt? All these problems are being faced and worked through. That is the way faith speaks. Yonggi Cho's faith is active and positive. When he was asking the Lord how he was to accommodate so many people, the Lord said to him, 'Well, you can't move out sideways but you can go up and you can go down.' With God nothing is impossible and it seems neither is it to Cho.

Experts have been called in to investigate the construction of an underground auditorium with three levels beneath the existing car park, to hold about 25,000 people. Then to extend the present building, it is planned to encircle it by another exterior wall, which, after demolition of the existing one, will expand the building to a seating capacity of 25,000. The new World Mission Building is just coming into use, a fine looking construction with goes thirteen floors up and three down. As the congregation grows new floors are pressed into service, each of which can accommodate 2,500 people.

Yonggi Cho's faith for growth involves him in actions of faith. Already he has reached out and possessed his half million, and is busily working in this incredible way to provide for them. With such an example of faith the people are whole-heartedly involved in the vision planting their mustard seed of faith which is blossoming and flourishing into a massive tree.

Faith for these huge things only comes from a childlike attitude to the Word of God and permeates down to affect every area of life. Through bible promises they have learned how to receive help for every contingency. In this way their faith grows and matures, and they possess health, success and prosperity in everything they do.

Their faith works through love, and is seen to do so in the whole network of the church's life, where the goal of their faith is love and not just success. Faith and love work in Central Church's thousands of committed Christians who are solidly rooted in the Word of God. Their love is not a passing sentiment but deep compassion for souls. The strong mixture of love and faith has welded a multitude of people together and produced the biggest church in the world.

8. *The Holy Spirit*

And God gives the increase The vital power for increase is the Holy Spirit himself. After considering all the principles expounded by Yonggi Cho and even wholeheartedly following them, there still will be no growth unless God steps in through the power of the Holy Spirit. No one is more conscious of his dependence on the Spirit than Yonggi Cho. His faith is not in his own abilities or the principles he has learned through hard experience over the years, but in God himself, by the power of the Holy Spirit. He actively honours the Holy Spirit, and lovingly welcomes Him to meetings. At one period he was so conscious that he dare not go before the people unless the Spirit was with him that symbolically he would leave the centre chair for Him. Yonggi Cho has a vital sense of co-operation with the Holy Spirit, of knowing that he is a co-worker with God. It's not just words, but is a controlling factor in his life. The determined self-motivated Cho of the past is very dead; today Yonggi Cho will do nothing unless he knows the companionship and prompting of the Holy Spirit every step of the way.

Obviously because the Holy Spirit is so honoured, loved, obeyed and respected in the fellowship of the church, he moves amongst them in power. Many mighty acts, miracles, signs, wonders and the other visible evidences of God's blessing in the church have caused its amazing growth. It is known that God is with the people and he appears to enjoy being there. Although the unconverted don't really understand, it is the Holy Spirit who is the central attraction. It's his peace, joy and love they feel when they walk through the door, it is the impact of his presence on their spirits which prompts many to acknowledge 'God is in this place.' It is his ministry of encouragement that assures them that their needs can be met. By the power of the Holy Spirit the church grows and grows.

Dealing with the masses

On average, seven to eight thousand people are added to the church each month. As you can imagine that means hundreds of new Sunday School teachers and house group leaders are also required month by month.

Every department of the church is discovering fresh leadership to involve in the expanding work. Each home group has an assistant who is being groomed to take half of the group, once it divides. Weekly the cell group leader fills in a small report on the meeting of how many people attended, the kind of response, and special note is made of those who could be prospective leaders for the future. They are recommended to the section heads who eventually interview them. If they fulfil the conditions of being full of faith, and full of the Holy Spirit, zealous and having a working knowledge of the Scriptures, they will be set apart as cell group leaders. Many of the same problems that we encounter occur there also. Sometimes they cannot find a new home cell leader and the group becomes too large whilst they wait. Thankfully though, most of their problems are only those of growth, and that's healthy. The young people's work is constantly looking for additional help. They too look for promising young men and women from within their own ranks whom they can promote. With such rapid growth naturally a strong emphasis is placed upon producing leadership.

I wondered how they managed to baptise so many believers. I could imagine someone developing huge muscles through immersing so many thousands! During the summer months they have mass baptismal services, when for days they continue baptising all the thousands who are waiting. Everyone in the church is exhorted to be baptised in water. The subject is clearly taught to all converts, although greater emphasis is laid upon baptism in the Holy Spirit. To become a member of Full Gospel Central Church is a leisurely affair. Time is given for the enquirer definitely to make up his mind in the light of knowledge after attending many meetings. After his initial response to the invitation in a meeting the enquirer is given an opportunity to complete a bible correspondence course. Lovingly the local house group follow up with an invitation to attend the home cell and other meetings at the main church. No compulsion is put upon a person to attend the new converts' class but they are made aware of it and encouraged to do so. Through the teaching in their cell and the class, they would be instructed in water baptism, the basics of the gospel and encouraged to reach out in faith to receive the baptism of the Holy Spirit. Tithing is also taught as one of the foundations. After about three months, if a person has been consistently growing in the Lord and obeying the teaching he has received, he will then be considered to be a member of the church and his name will go on to the permanent records. Each year these are reviewed and those who have failed in their commitment and attendance would have their names removed from the church records. Because of this level of diligence, the statistics of the church are fully trustworthy.

Prepared for anything

Because Seoul is only twenty-five miles from the demarcation line, the church is constantly aware of the communist threat. So many in the church have fresh memories of the horror of communist occupation and they are only too aware, in the climate of world events, how easily the whole thing could happen again. Boldly Yonggi Cho says, 'If the communists came into Seoul they would kill me and probably murder all the pastors. They could demolish the church buildings but they could never destroy the church.' The home cells are the strength of this church in Korea. They are spread throughout the city of Seoul and it would be impossible for any invader to fully discover and destroy them. Should such a catastrophe ever occur instructions have already been given that every record must first be destroyed. No evidence will be left for the enemy to decimate the church. The organisation is so large that no one person knows where all the cells are. To us that may sound rather dramatic, but South Korea lives in the reality of such a threat. Yonggi Cho sees the home cell system, which is so meshed in to the very fabric of society that it can resist even the most persistent pursuers, as God's answer for a persecuted church.

Cho's principles for growth have been discovered in the midst of life and activity. He has not followed them like instructions in a manual, but with a heart for God he has been led in their way. Now after years of experience he can confidently show the result; the largest church in the world.

FOUR

Squinting eyes and hard work

Success! I had managed to pick up a mouthful of kimchi with my chopsticks from the dish in the centre of the small table. Whilst my concentration was glued to landing it safely in my mouth before it dropped, my host studied my face. As I swallowed, he asked, 'Did you like the kimchi?' Really he was saying, 'Do you like Korea?', because kimchi and Korea are inseparable. It is as Korean as anything can be. Prepared by pickling chinese cabbage mixed with hot spices and sometimes other vegetables, it is eaten at almost every meal and enjoyed by everyone. Koreans frequently look for approval of their beautiful land of which they are naturally proud.

We can easily fail to realise how different Koreans are from their close neighbours in China and Japan. Despite a chequered history, Korea has managed to maintain an identifiable separate culture in which its people are very secure.

The past twenty years have brought many changes with increased wealth, modernisation and urbanisation. But unlike other places in the world, where rapid transition has blown the people about like flotsam, the Koreans have been successful in holding their society steady because their roots go down deeply into their culture. They have dealt gracefully with change and reaped its benefits, rather than allowing it to undermine them.

The Americans have been around in Korea for the best part of thirty years but surprisingly they haven't created a pseudo USA. It may be that their presence has contributed in a contrary fashion to the patriotism that most Koreans express. The National Anthem is sounded out over loud speakers daily at sundown, when the flags flying on many buildings are ceremonially lowered. Those within earshot stand still with their hands upon their hearts, wherever they are, till the music stops.

Oil and water

The lift stopped, the door was opened and I stepped in. The gentleman inside moved over and then bowed deeply to me. In the confined space there was hardly room and yet courtesy demanded he should greet me in this way. I endeavoured to do the same. As our western manners slowly infiltrate their public life, they present some problems. These days many people shake hands, but when they bow at the same time it usually ends up with them banging their heads!

Regardless of education or position in life, the old ways of thinking remain strong in the minds of most people. Some may be tempted to believe that Koreans are westernised because they have adapted to some of our customs of dress and manners, but they would be quite mistaken to assume that the outward appearance means that the inner aspirations and attitudes have changed. Western dress is far more convenient for jumping on and off buses or catching the subway, yet on any special occasion which requires best clothes and formality they naturally revert to their own. When walking in the streets one usually sees a sprinkling of those dressed in the old style. One does not need to go very far below the surface of everyday life to discover that Korea is still very Korean.

A woman's way

Today all children go to school; free education is available up to the elementary stage. Little girls sit in class with the boys and have the same opportunity, yet at home these same girls will be treated so very differently from their brothers. Most sons are hopelessly spoilt, whilst daughters are required to live sacrificial lives working and serving the whole family. Without too much trouble most young girls grow up to be women who accept a role where they serve their husband and family faithfully, whether appreciated or not. From their youngest days they are conditioned to that attitude.

The woman in Korea is always a follower, obeying her parents as a child, then after marriage her husband and, after his death, her eldest son. This traditional way of treating women is so woven into the very fabric of society that they expect nothing else. Perhaps it is this very attitude towards women that has caused them to develop very fine, noble characters, humble, hard working and unselfish. Their faithfulness to their family is expressed in a readiness to sacrifice. This may be one of the reasons why so many more women turn to Christ than men.

I watched the joyful face of Maria as she told me that next day she was to begin a new job in an office. She was the mother of a ten month old baby and expecting another child. She and her young husband, Kimil, lived with her father-in-law who was a cantankerous old man, but they were endeavouring to show him a Christ-like example that would turn his heart to the Lord. As Maria sang Christian songs to her baby and talked about the love of Jesus she hoped the old man overheard. Kimil, wishing to follow further theological study, left his job and went to work in Central Church's Education Department where he is engaged with others in translating a bible dictionary into Korean. He had been promised that after working there for one year he would be given a free place for postgraduate studies in theology, but because he was so anxious to get to college sooner his faithful wife offered to work and support him through college. In a selfless manner she was prepared to do anything to help her husband.

Fun-loving and cultured

The Plaza at Yoido on New Year's Day was covered with children tearing around on hired bicycles trying to thread their unpredictable way between others on roller skates, the experts weaving in and out while unsteady newcomers lurched from one catastrophe to the next.

It was a fun day, with whole families out enjoying themselves, and even the youngest were roller skating. Hanging on to mother on one side and dad on the other children not much bigger than toddlers were endeavouring to stay upright, while being dragged along. Cameras were clicking, recording charming pictures of children in national dress. The boys looked incongruous wearing highly coloured taffeta waistcoats, baggy sleeved shirts and equally baggy trousers, like jodphurs. The trousers were mostly of a bright lilac colour, teamed with red or emerald green waistcoats. The girls tore about in an ungainly fashion, hitching up their long gowns made from vivid coloured satins and silks. Underneath the children had layers of woolly clothing for despite the brilliant sunshine it was very cold. They seem content and secure, certainly loved and a joy to behold. All their baby years they are never far from mother; tied to her back they are so close as always to hear her heart beat. I wondered if that was the reason for their security.

In most middle-class families the children learn to play a musical instrument. Many of their ways of life are reminiscent of Victorian days. It is important to be accomplished and capable of entertaining at a moment's notice, and everybody is expected to be able to sing a song or make some contribution to a party. Visitors are not excepted. There is no place for modesty which says, 'Oh I don't think I could,' or 'I haven't got a very good voice.' A musical contribution is as normal to them as having a conversation.

When people meet socially, their conversation is not intended to give or receive information but to entertain. There is a certain formality in life which appears at first to be a little old fashioned.

Koreans are a cultured people, refined at heart, well acquainted with good music and with a deep respect of learning. I frequently encountered a touching reverence for natural beauty.

On summer days, instead of lying around on the grass in the parks, listening to transistors or just chatting, they carry their easels to an advantageous spot to paint and draw. Teenagers and people of all ages from the youngest to the oldest get busy with their water colours and oils, creating the most exquisite pictures. They are a most accomplished people. Besides playing musical instruments it seemed that almost every other person could paint beautiful views.

Westerners can seem very uneducated, totally oblivious to the demands of society for modesty and good taste. Stepping into this quaint world we could appear to be barbarians, blundering around in an uncouth blunt fashion unaware of the care that should be taken to observe the other person's feelings. Despite Korean etiquette, with its elaborate careful outward life, the people are openly emotional. They express their deep feelings, and will either weep or laugh in public quite easily. Even tears in a man are not considered a sign of weakness.

Certain national traits of character, together with the old religions, have influenced the whole nature of society in Korea. Koreans show themselves first of all to be a wonderfully adaptable people; various cultures have made their inroads into their lives and yet their ability to readjust has caused them to assimilate other ways and thoughts without the basic structure of their society being changed or shaken. Their flexibility has meant that they can put their arms around new things, take what is good and refuse that which does not appeal. Their patience as a nation has been demonstrated through many long periods of trial, and in individuals this same gentle patience is evident in many areas of life, although at the same time they are somewhat stubborn. Perhaps their common stubborness has preserved their Korean heritage, as they have resolutely resisted change which could have attacked the foundation of their society; at the same time, they have been flexible enough to welcome that which would do them good.

A religious soup

It has been said that Koreans are a people with no religion, that is to say, no organised religion. Buddhism came from China leaving its character in the land, but was overthrown by Confucianism. The Confucianist way which has left its ethos upon the culture is much more a philosophy than a religion, giving a love for learning the arts and a respect for knowledge. The most important Confucianist practice in Korean life today is the continuation of ancestral worship. Normally most Korean families make the annual pilgrimage to the grave mounds of their forefathers, where the eldest son will make sacrifices of food.

Alongside Confucianism and Buddhism, there is a Korean religion called Shamism, an animistic spirit religion with a priesthood. They teach a vague concept of salvation through a higher being, but their main activity is in endeavouring to control the spirits which they believe are in rocks, trees, earth and the sky. In times of sickness many turn to shamans, spirit mediums who are usually women, for assistance in driving out the evil spirits.

No one religion in Korea holds complete sway. Individuals are influenced by all of these religions, and are likely to turn to any particular one, according to his needs.

The Confucianist way of life has influenced the family structure, producing definite vertical relationships. Great respect is shown for the elderly, and the eldest son bears a deep sense of responsibility to uphold the honour and prestige of his family. Because families are such close-knit organisations they can work for or against the gospel. Many Korean villages have a family network of relationships sometimes covering half the village. If one person finds Christ it would soon become a whole family concern. At times this has meant that the individual has had to leave his family as Yonggi Cho did in his younger years, but it has worked gloriously in reverse when a positive decision has been made and entire groups have decided to follow Christ.

The bonds of relationship within the family groups are strong and authoritarian, which especially causes difficulty for women when they are the only converted Christian in the family.

Quiet and orderly

As we were finishing off a delicious meal a group of men came in and sat at a nearby table. The atmosphere of the restaurant was immediately jolted, their loud voices and raucous laughter causing everybody to turn and see. A Korean friend bent over and whispered in my ear, 'They are not Koreans, they are Chinese.' Up to that point I hadn't registered just how peaceful and quiet the restaurant was. Koreans are naturally very quietly spoken and in public places they do not draw attention to themselves.

We again notices their orderly behaviour when one hot afternoon as we struggled up the endless steps to the Namsan Tower we were passed by a group of young people dressed in green uniforms, on their way down. Carrying plastic bags and long aluminium tongs, they were picking up any sweet wrapper or match-stick that littered the path. These were part of a young people's organisation to keep Seoul tidy, volunteers who organise themselves into work parties to visit public places to keep them attractive and clean. Seoul is impressively clean and tidy, mainly because there is a general willingness in the ordinary person to put his rubbish in a bucket rather than throw it anywhere. It is all part of the orderly, submissive way of life.

Schoolchildren all wear uniforms and even young people going to colleges have distinctive clothing. There are many things in Korean life that express their corporate identity. Apart from uniforms, workers at particular factories and organisations can be identified by badges which are worn with a sense of pride in their button holes. Part of Korea's ability to lift itself effectively out of the economic devastation following the years of war has been the teachable, orderly way of life of the common man. The factory employee is a conscientious hard-working individual whose hours are incredibly long. Yet despite his small wages he is a faithful earnest worker, thankful to have a job.

Koreans are the perfect example of solid citizens.

The rose of Sharon is blooming

Korea's national flower is the rose of Sharon. Its simple form typifies the unsophisticated beauty of Korea and its people. As the flower blossoms and grows, so Christianity flourishes in the land. Apart from the Full Gospel Central

Church in Seoul, there are well over three thousand other churches in the city, and it is estimated that a new church opens in Korea every six minutes. The whole land is enjoying the breath of revival, in which there is an annual average of more than a million converts.

Central Church is a good example of the complete cross-section of society that is turning to Christ, although Seoul enjoys a far higher proportion of Christians than the national average.

Looking from the window of the train, as we travelled towards the east coast of Korea, we saw church buildings in every village and town we passed. Usually they were the largest building on the horizon, and often there were two or three in each community.

The church obviously benefits from Korea's national character traits. The diligent hard working factory worker becomes a faithful dedicated Christian. Their long working hours tend to make them value highly their limited free time which they use widely. The people hurry and often run; there is plenty to do in every precious moment.

Many of their right values in the traditional family relationships have become additional blessings to them since they have come to Christ. Father is certainly head of his home, and as a Christian he now takes the spiritual responsibility for his family. Daily he gathers his wife and children together to read the scriptures, praise God and pray. Their diligence to study and learn is now applied to their Christian lives. The children memorise the scriptures and are devoted to learning and understanding the bible.

English and learning

Pastor Lee told me that he wanted his children to inherit 'the invisible treasures', and so he spent time daily teaching them about the most important values in life: faith, truth and honesty. He also set about training each child to have a strong will which he considered to be their greatest asset because when yielded to God it is a powerful vehicle for faith.

Pastor Lee spends time talking to his children in English

every day. In school it is a compulsory subject but very few have any opportunity actually to speak it, therefore the pronunciation is usually abominable. But fluency in English is a most important asset and it will become even more so as Korea's trade relationships grow worldwide. The Christians, who have their eyes on the ends of the earth for purposes other than trade, also are exceptionally keen to learn English.

In Central Church there are a number of groups who meet together for English bible study to improve their pronunciation. For instance, Pastor Song spends every Sunday afternoon with those who want to learn how to greet the foreign visitors. Slowly they are learning by heart correct greetings and good answers to questions. As well as polite conversation, last year he memorised one hundred verses in English and his target for this year is three hundred. We laughed together as I sat in the class and corrected their pronunciation. Pastor Song's English class was a beautiful example of the dedicated application there is to learning; it is such a serious business but, unlike the old ways of Confucianism when learning itself was the goal, in Christ learning has become the means by which Christians can take the gospel to other lands. English for them is the key to travel; their motivation is world evangelism.

Pastor Song expressed his deep desire to serve God in communist China, so in addition to learning English verses by heart, he has set himself the target of one hundred verses in Chinese this year! He said, 'I fear no evil. My God is with me, and I believe he will take me one day to work in China.' While sitting with his group, listening to them read, my thoughts went to the communist cells which are sprinkled all over China. There the people gather, after long working hours, to fill their minds with communist propaganda, their solution to the world's needs. The fervour and love in the groups in Seoul where they come together to study so that they can take life to the millions in the world, goes far beyond the bounds of communist dedication.

A grass roots change

With thousands turning to Christ, they are encouraged to be even bolder in their witness. As they begin to understand the favour of God upon their own land, their call to world mission becomes a compelling force.

It is still less than one hundred years since the first resident missionaries came to Korea, and in that short space of time this little land has produced a Christian population which knows it has got something to give the whole world. This has done more for a people who had lost their self-respect and identity than anything else. A nation that was practically annihilated has now emerged as a mature people, with the answer to life. This sense of confidence and boldness colours their whole approach to witness.

Recently, a group of Koreans visiting a patient at the hospital were singing and praising God at his bedside. Turning to the man in the next bed they said, 'Are you a Christian? Would you like us to pray for you?' He replied that he was a Buddhist, but undeterred the Christians gathered round him and said, 'Our God loves you, and he will heal you too.' The man was so appreciative, and wanted their prayers. He knew the Christian's God heals; all that was necessary was that he should be introduced to him.

Gathered in the rows of seats at Central Church, Sunday by Sunday, are people moulded by their past culture and now transformed by the power of the gospel. Christ is not a veneer upon their old ways, but through the power of the Spirit, his life has seeped down into their origins.

The new bible culture

A transformation is taking place among the Christians where their Korean culture is being replaced by a new way of living. Without losing the benefits of that which is good, they are rapidly becoming those who follow a new bible culture. It has transformed the traditional attitudes to women. In Central Church we see a demonstration of a new way of living, which springs from a new way of thinking. Women who were once no more than chattels, or treated like animals, are now respected, joint heirs with Christ. In the families where father was feared and aloof, now in Christ he fulfils his role as true head of the home, a husband who loves his wife, cares for his children and takes responsibility for their moral and spiritual upbringing. Christ is touching the fabric of their society. In Christian homes boys can no longer be spoilt; now they too must learn to take responsibility, so that they will grow up to be good fathers and leaders in their homes and the nation.

Korea aspires to be a truly Christian nation. As this comes about the nationwide implementation of Christian standards of family life will prove to be a turning point in their history. It is not the westernisation of society that we look for but a cultural adjustment that will bring their whole way of life in line with the teaching of the bible. This is already happening and as it progresses even more rapidly in the years that are immediately ahead, brighter and brighter will become the power of the testimony coming from 'the land of the morning calm'. Could it be that in Korea, that small overlooked country, there is emerging a practical demonstration of what the Kingdom of God is really like on a national scale?

FIVE

The power supply

1 POWER THROUGH PRAYER

There is no need to look far to see the means of power for the church in Seoul. God has not changed his methods; they are the same good old fashioned ones that were used on the day of Pentecost. Truly the Koreans are a people who pray without ceasing. I have never met a people who pray so much. A gentleman, when offered a cup of coffee, bowed his head and fervently gave thanks. A beautiful view prompted immediate praise and hearts were lifted to the Lord, and when I arrived to visit a family thanks were immediately given that I had come at an opportune time. They are a people whose hearts are naturally turned to God. I wonder if naturally is the right word; they have trained themselves to be utterly dependent upon the Lord and have totally thankful hearts.

Any visitor to the church is immediately impressed by the quality of its prayer life. The people fervently pour out their hearts to God. At any gathering of the church the leader will pray for the nation, the church, the ministry of Christians worldwide and for the on-going power of the gospel in every country of the world. Although such prayers are repeated meeting by meeting, in no way are they a dead form because the people's hearts are genuinely involved.

A night out

Courting couples, mum and dad, and all the children shoving and pushing to get a seat for the all night prayer meeting! Have you ever heard of such a thing? It happens every Friday in the Full Gospel Central Church. The main auditorium soon fills up and then the front open area and aisles become crammed as the people spread themselves on the floor and in any odd corner. In another over-flow hall the young people have their own special all night prayer meeting. By nine-thirty in the evening buses from all over the city begin to roll in and look for a place to park. The people run to get a seat and then wait until ten o'clock when the service begins. One of the pastors takes his place on the rostrum and leads the enthusiastic singing with hand-clapping. Joyfully the people praise the Lord.

I joined the crowd and had to wait at the barrier where people were being turned away because there were no more seats in the balconies. The determination to get through was more like the crowd at the summer sales in Oxford Street. Patiently the ushers directed the people to different entrances and I was allowed to slip past them and up the stairs into the balcony, where I could hear a translation of the main evening message.

As I took my seat there was a tingling atmosphere of expectation in the air, more akin to a night at the Proms than a prayer meeting. A buzz of excitement was going through the crowd. I squeezed on to the end of a pew next to a family; mother, father and two daughters. The youngest girl was about thirteen, and kindly wriggled out of her seat and sat on the step of the balcony next to me to make room.

From my vantage point in the balcony I couldn't help but laugh, as I watched a very energetic, elderly lady surreptiously slip past the ushers to look for a good place at the front of the meeting. She sat down squarely in the middle of the aisle and had to be moved on by the ushers, tactfully but firmly. They reminded me of London 'Bobbies' at times.

There were mothers with babies tied to their backs, doing their best to jog them off to sleep before the meeting began. It looked so uncomfortable for both the baby and the poor mother, who for most of the time was half bent over, trying to pacify a wriggly, heavy load which objected to being squashed up in a crowd.

Dr Paul Yonggi Cho

Left: Full Gospel Church at Sodaemoon

Below: The Tent Church at Daejo Dong where it all began in 1958

Full Gospel Central Church, Yoido. Though it is full seven times every Sunday, less than half the membership can be accommodated

Full Gospel Central Church, Yoido

1. Memorial Gymnasium 2. Victory Hall 3. Main Auditorium 4. Ten storey Education Building
5. New sixteen storey World Mission Centre

At ten the meeting began with a lusty Korean translation of 'There is power in the blood of the Lamb', quickly followed by 'Whiter than snow', and 'Have you been to Jesus for his cleansing power?' There was nothing mechanical in the singing, everybody joining in with body, soul and spirit. After a chorus written by Yonggi Cho, which seemed to be a favourite, he led the people in prayer. I have never felt so drawn out in my spirit to pray for a land and its leaders as I was that evening. Yonggi Cho lifted his voice and his prayer came from the depths of his spirit, crying for God to bless his land, the President and members of Parliament. He longed for them all to be converted and baptised with the Holy Spirit. Continuing, he prayed that such a wealth of blessing should come upon Korea that out of her prosperity she would be able to send the Word of God worldwide. Earnest supplication was made that Korea should be united, not through warfare, but by the power of the Holy Spirit. With so many of them having their roots in North Korea, they prayed that the Holy Spirit would work in the hearts of the people there to strengthen and encourage them. Yonggi Cho then invited the whole congregation to pray unitedly. There was no stopping them as with a noise like thunder twelve thousand hearts, so open for God to move, poured out their supplications. All round me they were crying, some sobbing. It was only when a bell was rung that the people stopped praying.

As they quietened and wiped the tears from their faces they stood up and repeated the Apostle's creed. At every meeting, even in the cell groups this is said, probably as a means of teaching the foundations of the faith to the thousands of new believers.

Once again the vast company raised their voices, this time to sing 'Since I have been redeemed', and then Yonggi Cho came forward to speak. At the Friday night prayer meeting two messages are preached, one of them usually by Pastor Cho. His subject that evening was, 'What is the full gospel?'

The church had been criticised by those who said, 'they

only speak in tongues and pray for the sick, and as there are doctors we have no need for miracles today.' Encouraging his people, he showed them from the scriptures that Jesus did miracles, and said that we should not be ashamed to ask for miracles or perform them in the name of Jesus. He is the same yesterday, today and forever. Enthusiastically he called them to believe the Word of God: 'Jesus has died and has risen; he has borne away our sins, taken the curse for everyone of us, redeemed us from poverty and sickness. The baptism in the Holy Spirit is God's gift for every believer. You can be delivered from every bondage and demon. Jesus is the answer. The full gospel meets every need!'

Teaching slowly and carefully Cho built one principle upon another. He encouraged them afresh to reach out and be baptised in the Holy Spirit. 'There were only one hundred and twenty Christians on the day of Pentecost but when they were baptised with the Holy Spirit they went everywhere, empowered to do the works of God and to perform miracles. And now,' he says, 'look, it has gone all over the world.'

'Don't be fearful of the opposition. Even in bible days Jesus was criticised, and it was said of him that he did the works of the devil, but when opposition came he didn't stop. He continued to do the will of his father. Now you are the disciples of Jesus. In times of difficulty and persecution don't worry or be concerned. Jesus is coming. It's the time to proclaim his victory to the world. Our God fights for us, so don't be afraid of the works of the devil. We have overcome them in the name of Jesus. In the last days, the bible says, many will follow false teachers and false prophets, but you follow hard after the truth of the Word of God.'

The atmosphere in the meeting was as if a father stood in the middle of his family explaining simply to them how to handle false accusations when they didn't understand. His spirit was so loving and forgiving, like a father putting his strong arms around his children to protect his own.

Prayer requests received from all round the world were

on the table, and placing his hands on them Dr Cho pleaded that by the power of the Spirit every prayer would be answered for those who had written. Everyone prayed until the bell rang. Many testimonies of God's immediate answer to these prayer requests are brought to the church at each meeting. By this time it was well past twelve o'clock. We all stood up and stretched ourselves as we sang another rousing hymn proclaiming the simple truths of the gospel. As I looked about me, there were people standing at the back of the balconies, behind the choir seats and on the steps leading down to the orchestra area. Many stood the whole night through.

A change of activity came as we were led in exercises to wake us up! Stretching our arms to the right and then to the left, the whole congregation responded, reaching as high as we could. There was no room to bend down and touch our toes but we all followed as Yonggi Cho ran on the spot and jumped! Then came action choruses of the most vigorous kind with everybody participating and thoroughly enjoying themselves.

We all resumed our places as different subjects were put before us and unitedly lifted to God, one after another. All the praying was in unison. The volume of noise was tremendous. About me the people were totally absorbed, as with arms outstretched and voices raised they poured out their hearts to God, many with tears running down their faces. The young girl sitting on the step next to me was as involved as the mature saints. The roar of prayer continued with each new request until the bell rang. The praying was interspersed by singing and before I realised an hour had fled past.

If quantity of prayer means anything, many thousands of prayer hours had been lifted to God before we left the meeting. The type of activity and the leadership of the meeting changed every hour. First united worshipping and praising, then preaching and some praying, followed by a concerted hour of prayer punctuated by songs. There was a further message from one of the elders, and then at about three a.m. many people came forward to share their testimonies. I could see an embarrassingly large number wanting to speak. The ushers quickly sorted them out and one by one, in the most detailed and lengthy fashion, they told of their answers to prayer. Interspersed by a beautiful solo, chorus singing and times of rejoicing in prayer, the testimonies continued till twenty to four in the morning. Then the meeting was drawn to a close, and by four o'clock we were filing down the stairs into the early morning darkness. The buses were still waiting; the people piled in to go back to their homes for an hour or two's sleep before they left for work in the morning.

Every night there is an all night prayer meeting where a few hundred will gather, but Wednesday and Friday are special times. Often Pastor Cho is present for the Friday meeting, but leaves after he has preached. The Wednesday meetings are not programmed the same way and are not so large. On average 2,000 people gather to pray for their personal needs especially those seeking to be baptised in the Holy Spirit.

At the crack of dawn

Early morning meetings for prayer begin at four thirty a.m. and are a regular practice in Korean churches all over the country, where people of most denominations gather, often in large numbers.

At Central Church there is a regular early morning prayer meeting in one of the chapels and additional halls are rented throughout the city to avoid having to travel to Yoido at that time of day. As the church grows so the prayer ministry grows too, and extra space is constantly being provided as new earnest pray-ers are added to the congregation.

The converts from Buddhism, Shaminism and other religions need instruction in Christian prayer. They are used to pleading with hopeless persistence before their gods, a mode of prayer which is an integral part of false religion. So by careful teaching they are re-educated in their approach to God. First they must put away hopeless pleading, then come to their loving heavenly Father in faith, knowing that he delights to meet his people and all their needs. For many of these simple converts it takes time for them to understand the goodness of God, and perhaps their way of prayer initially may not be perfectly right, yet God who looks upon the heart knows how sincere and committed they are.

Prayer at Central Chuch is definite, aimed at specific needs and linked with preaching which clearly lays the foundation of the gospel of grace in the people's lives. Prayer, backed up with the Word of God and mixed with faith, brings the people into God's presence where they can simply, like little children, receive all their needs.

Added together the number of hours spent in prayer is enormous, ascending from one group or another almost continuously throughout the week. Women are predominant in the early morning and all night prayer meetings and for many intercession is their major ministry. These faithful nobodies regularly win mighty victories in the heavens and by their prayers power is released into the life of the church. Only God knows what they accomplish day by day and night by night.

With thanksgiving

I was challenged by their faithful obedience to the scripture, 'First of all, then, I urge that supplications, prayers, intercessions, and thanksgivings be made for all men, for kings and all who are in high positions, that we may lead a quiet and peaceable life, godly and respectful in every way. This is good, and it is acceptable in the sight of God our Saviour, who desires all men to be saved and to come to the knowledge of the truth' (1 Tim. 2:1–4). At almost every meeting they pray in this manner, which has an interesting effect upon their attitude to their government. It isn't all that could be desired, but because of their prayer involvement they are loyal citizens who trust God to work through their elected representatives. Wholeheartedly they accept the institution of their government as by the will of God and for the nation's good. The National Assembly is within walking distance of the church and is under the permanent influence of its prayers.

Thankfulness is a beautiful attitude, encouraged in all the prayers and expressed with joy when answers are received as they listen to testimonies of God's goodness. A strong source of power has been tapped by simple people who persist in thankfulness.

The bible has many injunctions about prayer which they delight to obey. They are persistent and sincere; they come in a unity of spirit, agreeing together that these things shall be so: they do not forget to come; they pray always and do not faint, with strong intercessions and supplication for their leaders; they pray in the Spirit and with understanding. There is not one command of scripture concerning prayer that they do not obey. Coming in faith, bringing their requests to their Father who delights in his children, their prayers have touched a power supply which can never be exhausted.

I have described such a vigorous prayer life that you must wonder if the people ever go to sleep! Here's where numbers win – thousands sleep every night in their own beds whilst others are at prayer vigils, standing against the powers of darkness and calling down the blessing of God. In fact only a very small percentage of the whole church is usually present on any one occasion at the variety of prayer meetings available.

A visit to prayer mountain

Winter days in Seoul are sunny but very cold and dry. As I went down the steps of the World Mission Building a long line of people stood in the bright sunshine. Men and women, teenagers, people from all walks of life waited with their small bundles of belongings to board the bus to take them to Prayer Mountain. I went to take their photograph. It was the Lunar New Year, a public holiday. Rather than honour it in the traditional way by worshipping the spirits of the dead, these families and individuals had chosen to devote the day to God in fasting and prayer. Their dedication overwhelmed me, since the New Year holiday is normally celebrated with special food and family gatherings where they wear national dress. It is an occasion among non-Christians when the young people solemnly bow to their elders to show respect.

Dr Cho says one of the main factors in the growth of Full Gospel Central Church was the establishing of Prayer Mountain in 1973 by his mother-in-law, Dr Jashil Choi. It is a mountain only in the sense that it is where people go up to meet God. Situated at Osanri, about one hour's journey north of Seoul in the hills, it is the church's prayer retreat.

On my first visit I received a warm welcome from the pastor in charge. We slipped off our shoes and were shown into his office. The heated floor felt good under foot. No matter where I went in this huge church, even in this hill retreat centre, there were crowds of people and a very busy staff. A girl served us with ginseng tea, a Korean speciality made from a root with the supposed property of prolonging life.

We had come for the afternoon meeting. During the day there are four meetings with teaching, ministry and prayer. When the place is full the congregation meets in five different chapels with a combined capacity of 15,300 but that afternoon about 3,000 were gathered. Sitting on the floor were mothers with babies on their backs, and men and women of all ages.

The vast number were sincere Christians with the light of the Lord evident upon their faces but among them were the obviously ill, the demon possessed, the crippled and handicapped, who had come seeking a miracle. They were at the right place. Prayer Mountain is renowned for miracles. Countless stories are told of those who have been healed or who have seen God's intervention in impossible situations.

I stepped up on to the platform where I was to speak to the crowd who had gathered. They were seated on the floor, bundled up in blankets, many wearing layers of jumpers. Just in front of me was a very ill man lying on a makeshift bed. I shared my testimony and then the Pastor led in prayer. A young man from Kenya, another visitor, then preached the Word of God with power. Whilst he was speaking a demon screamed out and a man was taken to the back of the hall, where some helpers prayed for him.

As soon as the meeting drew to its close the people responded to the message. They thronged to the front wanting the preacher to pray for them. A crippled boy was being walked about the platform; one demon had already yelled out but now many others were obvious. We left the hall and the resident pastors took over.

Pushing through the crowd of people in the outer office who were seeking deliverance, we made our way inside the pastor's room where we sipped another cup of ginseng tea from small delicate china cups. Outside we could hear demons yelling as they were being cast out. Prayer Mountain is not a place for a picnic; it's the front line of spiritual warfare.

Sister Choi, the founder, led this work, preaching and praying for people daily until recently. Her wisdom and advice is constantly sought by those who suffer and long for God to answer their prayers. Wherever persistent problems are met in the life of believers pastors always encourage the people to fast as well as pray. Through this mighty weapon, many entrenched problems are solved, demons cast out and sicknesses healed. An uncommonly large number of cancer patients find complete healing through prayer and fasting. Dr John Hurston said, 'Prayer, with fasting, is a way of life in Central Church.'

Apart from its effectiveness in these situations the weapon of fasting with prayer is powerfully wielded against the powers of darkness to deliver thousands from its kingdom; like incense, continual prayer is offered for the church, its ministries, for Korea and the whole world. The church's growth, and the continuation of the outpouring of the Holy Spirit in the whole of Korea flows from a depth of prayer identification with the suffering Saviour that few of us understand.

The duration of a person's stay at Prayer Mountain varies. For some it is day visit, while others go for prolonged fasts, even as long as forty days. Normally however fasts are for three days to a week.

All the different departments and organisations in the church arrange periodic retreats. The date is announced and the whole company take the bus to Prayer Mountain for its own particular kind of intimate fellowship.

At present the crowds are accommodated in a huge tent meeting hall while a permanent prayer sanctuary for 10,000 is under construction.

Besides the communal meetings for ministry and prayer, when requests from worldwide are lifted to God, there are individual prayer closets for those who want to be alone.

Throughout the day fresh bus loads arrive. The charter bus service runs every hour from the forecourt of the church.

'In 1980, 86,785 visits were made to Prayer Mountain for the express purpose of fasting and prayer. Half these came to receive the Baptism in the Holy Spirit, one out of every six for physical healing and the remainder for a variety of reasons. It is interesting to note that almost two thirds of those who came for extended times of prayer and fasting are from other churches all over Korea as well as Seoul. A staff of full-time pastors and lay people, altogether one hundred and thirty workers, are daily involved in the ministry.'[1]

A few days after my first visit I joined the line, in the biting wind, to board the bus to go again to Prayer Mountain. We took our seats, and through a loud speaker system the driver gave a few words of explanation and encouragement, then led us all in prayer. As we drove out of the forecourt a tape was put on and we were accompanied by choruses for the whole journey.

People from each fresh bus load register at the office and are issued with a plastic bag bearing the picture of Prayer Mountain. These bags are provided for shoes which are removed once inside the meeting halls because the people sit and sleep on the floors. Everyone walks around with their plastic bag, almost the badge of Prayer Mountain.

I was shown into a fine building housing more than 350

people in dormitory accommodation, although this is quite inadequate of course to cater for everyone staying at Prayer Mountain. Then I went for a tour of the whole site. The majority live in the five meeting halls and as we picked up a tent flap I saw families camped together in a mass of blankets to keep themselves warm while they fasted and prayed in sub-zero temperatures.

After seeing the crowds I understood why I was especially shown the prayer grottos. These are tiny rooms like little cubes, only about five foot in each direction with not enough height to stand up in, totally bare except for a kneeling mat on a slightly warm floor. There one can be alone to pray. As we walked past people were crying out to God from behind the little closed doors. The rooms were in great demand and many would remain there the whole night in prayer; not quite the western idea of comfort.

I was taken to visit the elder in charge of all the ministry at Prayer Mountain. This kindly looking gentleman handed me a copy of 'Fasting Prayer' a regular publication with articles and testimonies of those who had been healed. They have an endless supply of amazing stories of God's intervention which are printed and distributed to encourage faith.

Miss Yong Okay Eum is twenty-four years old. In November 1978 she had a serious nose bleed while sleeping. The following day it continued and discharged a foul smelling fluid. Full of fear she hurried to the hospital. When the doctor examined her he advised an immediate operation. Unable entirely to trust one doctor's word she went to another hospital where she had an X-ray. The consultant held the film up to the light and pointed to a cancer in the brain. 'I'm sorry to tell you that surgery is of no value, the tumour has gone too far. You have only a short time to live!'

Fearfully she visited many hospitals but no-one could help her, and soon all hope was gone.

As a last resort her mother went to the fortune tellers who advised her to employ an exorcist. Three Shamans, women like witch doctors, were brought to the home to conduct their evil ceremonies. They poured hot water upon her, burned her with coins and beat her with rods. The Shamans thought by these means to drive the demons out of Miss Yong. Of course nothing brought her any relief, she waited to die.

Neighbours knew her terrible plight and told the local Methodist pastor who visited and prayed. There was only one prognosis: she would die, unless God did a miracle.

'Why don't you go to Prayer Mountain? God does miracles there,' urged the pastor.

They were a Buddhist family but in their desperation were ready to take his advice. The parents took their daughter, whose illness had become so serious that she was almost too weak to walk, for a prolonged visit to Prayer Mountain. She was supposed to have medicine every two hours but was unable to keep it down. Her parents nursed her and as she was too weak to pray, they decided to pray and fast for her recovery themselves. After three days the mother had a vision of a blue cross. The next day she saw a white cross and at the same time Miss Yong's nose stopped discharging. For the first time in months she could breathe through her nose and her sense of smell began to return. The fast continued and on the seventh day her mother saw a red cross. The young woman who over the months had become deaf suddenly found she could hear again. The family continued with another two weeks of fasting and prayer, and then went home. Three months later Miss Yong Okay Eum had completely recovered, and the whole family with all their relatives became believers.

There are many testimonies of non-Christians who have gone to Prayer Mountain in utter despair, with fasting and prayer they have sought God, been saved, and received a miracle from the Lord.

Another story is told about Mrs Yong Ja Kim. She lives in Seoul, and in September 1981 was diagnosed to have cancer in her uterus. Her husband and whole family were Buddhists, and although she had believed in Jesus some years earlier she had never been regularly to church as there was always too much trouble and misunderstanding in her home.

She became very ill but the family were heartless, caring nothing about her condition. No one even tried to understand. Some Christians encouraged her to go to Prayer Mountain to fast for three days but although she went she had no faith that she could recover. In the meetings many people made a lot of noise and others prayed in tongues. She couldn't understand what was happening and felt lonely and ill, so she went home.

Early next day she went to the morning service at a local church. There her sister, who had become a Christian, encouraged her to return to Prayer Mountain. This time accompanied by her sister and a pastor she stayed and prayed, and after several hours she felt the burden of sin so great upon her that she repented in a loud voice, raising her hands. Joy filled her heart, and she knew her sins were really forgiven. Then the Spirit of God fell upon her and she spoke in tongues as she was baptised in the Holy Spirit. Peace and joy flowed within her.

Mrs Kim continued to fast for another two days and then went home. Feeling better in her body she wondered whether to go to her doctor, as she wanted him to confirm her healing. Another church member said, 'Don't test God, just believe', so she waited. After a few weeks had passed she decided to go to the hospital where a doctor examined her. With a puzzled look he pronounced her totally healed, and said, 'And where did you get this healing?'

'I went to Prayer Mountain; my good God has made me perfect.'

Now she is praying for the doctor and her family. Testimonies like these abound. Prayer Mountain is understandably renowned for the works of power, signs, wonders and miracles accomplished there.

The cost of fasting

During my visit it was extremely cold, which strangely helped me to understand a little more about the sufferings of Christ. At best when fasting one feels the cold, yet despite the extra trial of the low temperatures there I met people determined to carry their prayer burden through. Hot water would have been a small comfort but they only drank it cold. When I looked into the faces of those obviously having prolonged fasts, I hurt inside. Pondering my own reaction I knew it was my flesh recoiling from the pain that they experienced. They were living like well dressed refugees without food, sharing a floor with hundreds of others in the same condition. At anytime they could have gone home to food, warmth and comfort but they chose to remain.

In a manner, those fasting in this way are declaring their readiness to die to see their prayers answered. It is not an attempt to blackmail God but a total identification with the sufferings of Christ to bring about his will and purpose. They are standing with God against the powers of darkness. By their actions they say, 'Whether I live or whether I die, I'll see this thing through.' They have brought their bodies under the control of the Spirit and of course it has its outworking in every area of their lives. They have become a Spirit-controlled people.

Jashil Choi taught a pattern of fasting in which each fast is divided into three periods. The first is spent in repentance and seeking forgiveness from all sin. Then specific requests are brought before the Lord. Persistently they pray for hours, yearning, longing, interceding that God will meet their need. The answer to the prayer does not signal an immediate end to the fast, but instead a time of thanksgiving, the third period, in which their gratitude is offered with another day of fasting.

You may wonder who all these people are who have so much time to spend in prayer and fasting. Obviously for those who are sick and unable to work it is the best place to be, while others may take a week of their annual leave. For the majority, however, it is a day's event squeezed in among the many busy activities of life. Quite a number of people make a visit to Prayer Mountain as a last resort after every other channel of prayer and intercession has been exhausted.

For instance, when Mrs Lee's husband became a full-time pastor it was necessary for them to move house to be nearer to the church. However it appeared that their large old house in a suburb of Seoul would never sell, and even the money they thought they could raise on it would be insufficient to buy one of the modern flats in Yoido. All discussion had come to an end without any answer to their problem.

Then Mrs Lee announced that she would go to Prayer Mountain to fast and pray for five days. God would show them what to do. She packed her things and went.

On the fourth day of her fast her husband had a visitor at home. It was the neighbouring hotel keeper, who cautiously asked him if he would be prepared to sell his property as he wanted to enlarge his premises. The deal was settled before Pastor Lee's wife came home the next day and within weeks the right property, close to the church and at a good price, was located. How happy the family were to know God's special provision and care for them as they moved into a new sphere of ministry.

The church's businessmen's association became involved in helping in a government training scheme for the rehabilitation of ex-prisoners. Of course their only answer for these former thieves and pick-pockets was to take them to Prayer Mountain for a period of 'training'. I imagine that their few days in the country have had a life-long effect! Prayer forms a dynamic hidden structure within every department of the life of the church. It is as natural as breathing, and considered as essential. It is through prayer the whole body remains vitally alive.

2. POWER THROUGH TITHING

Understandably you may wonder why I have included a section on tithing in a chapter about power. Who would have thought that giving releases power? In Central Church, tithing comes into the same category as prayer with fasting, both are an essential way of living. Tithing is not a law or membership rule in the church but a wise decision made in the light of the promises of God by thousands of the members. None is under any obligation to tithe but the majority joyfully do, for to them giving is a principle of life.

Poverty is not blessed

Almost everyone in Korea understands poverty. As a nation and as individuals they are successfully pulling their feet out of its mire and no one wishes to return there. Koreans will work very long hours and do anything rather than suffer again for want of food and the basic necessities of life. They are a diligent, hard working people, quite uncomplaining about their lot in life, probably because poverty is only just over their shoulder.

Of course there are the poor who have difficulty in making ends meet, and the majority don't enjoy the luxuries of life that we take for granted. The average standard of living provides housing, clothes and basic food where meat would appear about twice a week on the menu. It's an expensive item. But compared to India, where I have lived for many years, Korea is a prosperous nation.

Yonggi Cho said, 'God never created poverty; it was never his intention that his people should be poor. He made the Garden of Eden absolutely lush and overflowing with abundance. Everything that man could need was there in a most lavish generous supply.

'Poverty came with sin. When Adam and Eve sinned they were cast out of the garden and away from the luxury of God's rich bounty. By the sweat of his brow Adam was to provide for his family in a continual battle against thorns and thistles, year in and year out.'

Lifting up his voice Pastor Cho declared, 'But Chirst has borne the curse for us; he has set us free from the curse of sin, death and poverty. "For you know the grace of our Lord Jesus Christ, that though he was rich, yet for your sake he became poor, so that by his poverty you might become rich" ' (2 Cor. 8:9).

Yonggi Cho teaches that deliverance from poverty is

included in our whole salvation. The deliverance we have received in Jesus is completely sufficient to cover every area of our lives. As we submit our wills and give up our sins, we receive eternal life. It is an act of faith: without any idea of what the future holds, we step out and trust our Saviour.

In a similar way, giving one tenth of all I have back to God is also an act of faith where I declare, 'Lord I'm trusting you for my future prosperity, my standard of living, my everyday needs and the unexpected extra demands; I'm not going to be my own saviour, I'm trusting your faithfulness. I believe your word.' Giving a tenth is like planting a seed of faith which bears the promise of fruitfulness.

Tithing has become such a blessing to Full Gospel Central Church that they cannot keep quiet about it. Anyone in financial trouble will soon hear of the benefit of obeying God's principles in giving. It's a crazy paradox: if you want to have enough and to spare, take what you have and give generously, then God will supply all your need.

The way up is down

Mr Ki Yong Lee is a businessman in Seoul. Over the past four years his small manufacturing concern got into financial difficulties. He was quickly heading for bankruptcy and day and night was worrying himself sick. Although a Buddhist he decided to go to church to ask God for help. He began to attend every Sunday, then added the Wednesday and Friday night prayer meetings, where he heard testimonies from believers telling of the blessings received through tithing. He decided tithing was the answer to his problem but he had no regular money, so whatever little he got he gave.

With all hope extinguished, he decided to go to Prayer Mountain where he planned to fast for three days. As the time drew to an end he decided to continue for another three. Still he had no hope for the business; his factory lay idle and his workers were laid off.

In his muddled thinking he went to enlist the prayers of

his mother, as he considered they would be very powerful. She prayed continuously, but as a devout Buddhist. He planned to preach the gospel to her so that she would believe and pray to the Christian God. Unfortunately she was most unresponsive!

Suddenly light seemed to appear on his gloomy horizon. A relative asked him to join in a business partnership for which he would require ten thousand pounds, but of course Mr Lee had nothing. Snatching at straws he borrowed one hundred and fifty pounds from his mother, which he immediately gave to God as a seed of faith. Then he set himself to pray till an answer came, but the situation only got blacker and blacker. A creditor for some years back appeared at his home and demanded money or he would take him to court. Mr Lee begged for time to pay. Then the relative who had offered the partnership proposition backed out and Mr Lee was left again with no prospect for the future.

Filled with anxiety and fear the poor man didn't know which way to turn, so once again he went to Prayer Mountain, this time to fast for ten days. He had no other hope but God.

A few days later he had a vision in which he saw a mountain of gold and silver. His spirit rose, and convinced that the answer was on the way he praised God and continued to fast to the end. When he arrived back in Seoul a huge order from a new client awaited him, providing a turning point in his finances. For Mr Lee it was a miracle.

Full Gospel Businessmen's Fellowship

Mr Lee is now a member of the Full Gospel Businessmen's Fellowship where he serves God with the abundance he has been given. After God brought him through that dark period he gave a large thank offering by which he was saying to God, 'Everything I have is yours.'

Many have been drawn into the Businessmen's Fellowship when near to bankruptcy. The testimonies of successful businessmen who tithe have goaded them to seek God. Hopeless men on the verge of despair and suicide have had their whole lives transformed when converted, finding that God puts their business in order and causes them to prosper beyond their wildest dreams.

The desire for prosperity among these men is not for themselves. They wish to give of their abundance to help many humanitarian causes and the worldwide evangelistic outreach of the church. So many of them grew up poor and struggled to get a basic education. Now through their prosperity, besides many other good works, they help children in a similar plight.

The F.G.B.F. at Central Church is not affiliated to the international organisation, the only reason for this being that the men want all their effort and money to be used in their own local church to expand its ministries, which cover a vast field.

The men have divided themselves into, currently, eleven associations, each concentrating its efforts in a particular way. Four are purely for missionary outreach into different continents. One provides finance to spread the gospel through mass media, radio and television. Others have concentrated their efforts into church buildings in Korea, especially for men in the Army and their families. Others with professional skills provide their services free. The extent of their activities is far ranging, all expressing their desire to give. Providing their services is not a substitute for their money; they are giving themselves freely in addition to their tithes and offerings.

In their offices and factories the workers have organised meetings for prayer and preaching, many being led to the Lord in this way. The working conditions of the people are improved as Christian employers seek to do the will of God in every area of their lives.

Tithing begins when people first offer themselves freely to the Lord. F.G.B.F. is a beautiful example of how God intends us to function.

Get your motives right

To talk openly about financial needs some might consider carnal. But the fact remains that for years the work of God has been crippled through lack of finance. The church has presented an image of always being hard-up, always fund raising, always pushing the plate under the nose of reluctant givers. 'All they want is our money!' say many non-church goers. In truth it may appear that way. Often the only notice outside a church is an appeal for funds, or an announcement of a jumble sale to repair the roof. With so many buildings in a state of neglect and decay, we can't blame the world if it doesn't believe 'all silver and gold belongs to our God.' The life style of the average church hardly declares to a cynical world that God is blessing his people, but Hallelujah, in these days things are changing. There is a growing number of churches scattered throughout the land where the tithes and offerings are faithfully given. They now experience the abundance of God and their prosperity is seen.

Many may question the ethics of their kind of giving. Yonggi Cho rightly says, 'God does not give lasting blessings to those with selfish desires.' A 'giving to get' attitude never receives God's approval. He still looks upon the heart and it is from there he judges a man's actions. When teaching about giving Yonggi Cho's first injuctions are to the hearts of his hearers and not to their pockets. 'Seek first the kingdom of God and don't worry about material needs. All the rest will be added to you if you've got the first thing right.' He plainly exhorts the people to give God first place in their hearts and lives, and then to give their time and money. Offering yourself to God is living a life completely dependent upon the Holy Spirit.

Much of our society today is motivated by greed. It is a sin common to those who have as well as those who have not. The industrial strife and strikes with which we live are a symptom of how deep the infection of greed has gripped men's hearts today.

It is true to say that whatever spirit prevails in the world will attempt to influence the church. Unfortunately greed and envy have filtered into the attitudes of many Christians. The bible warns us that love of money is the root of all evil. When people give with greed hidden in their hearts, thinking they will get in return, they are completely deceived. Giving to God springs from an entirely different motive.

We can safely live according to the scripture which says, 'God has promised to supply all our needs.'[2] Obviously these differ worldwide. The needs which together make our kind of society are legitimate for us. God is the judge of where need becomes greed.

One sure way to arrive at acceptable attitudes to money and prosperity is to say, 'Everything I have, Lord, belongs to you.' Lift your open hand to God, and mentally put everything on it; your money, opportunities, prosperity, assets and everything you are. Say, 'Lord, I am giving it to you. You can take it all away and I won't complain, or you can leave it with me and I will be a good steward by your grace. I'll thank you for these things Lord. I will not call them mine; all is yours.'

If we have that kind of heart, God can trust us with plenty, can trust us to be a channel for his money. It won't get clogged down in our pockets, or gum up our spirits with covetousness and the love of money.

All that we have belongs to the Lord, not just the tithe. He wants to provide for us generously and will delight to give us as much as we can handle, as long as it doesn't pervert and spoil us. God looks for those whom he can prosper, so that he can make his money flow through those trustworthy channels to finance the kingdom of God in these vital days.

Investing in a blessing

One tenth, or as the bible says, the tithe, is taught in the church as the basic level of giving. It does not originate from the Mosaic law as some think. Abraham gave tithes before the law was instituted. Throughout scripture God links tithing with prosperity: 'Honour the Lord with your substance and with the first fruits of all your produce; then your barns will be filled with plenty, and your vats will be bursting with wine' (Prov. 3:9, 10).

'Bring the full tithes in to the storehouse, that there may

be food in my house; and thereby put me to the test, says the Lord of Hosts, if I will not open the windows of Heaven for you and pour down for you an overflowing blessing. I will rebuke the devourer for you, so that it will not destroy the fruits of your soil; and your vine in the field shall not fail to bear, says the Lord of Hosts. Then all nations will call you blessed, for you will be a land of delight, says the Lord of Hosts' (Mal. 3:10–12).

The congregation are taught to take the scriptures at face value to follow what John Hurston calls a way to irreversible prosperity. As the church has grasped the concept of tithing, thousands have walked out of their poverty and are now prosperous. They firmly believe that to obey the scriptures will bring its promises upon them and their land.

They are generous, spontaneous givers, tithing joyfully and giving thank offerings. They have proved the truth of: 'Give, and it will be given to you; good measure, pressed down, shaken together, running over, will be put into your lap. For the measure you give will be the measure you get back' (Luke 6:38). It seems to be a universal law that the givers are blessed ones. When God created the world he put the Sea of Galilee and the Dead Sea side by side, like a parable of life. The Dead Sea receives but never gives and all around is death; the Sea of Galilee flows out to satisfy a broad river, while its own waters abound with fish and everywhere around its shores is life.

Out of his own generous heart has flowed a ministry by which Yonggi Cho has produced a church full of such enthusiastic givers that now they have the reputation of being prosperous. Economically the country suffers with high inflation, and the percentage of unemployed is in double figures, but those who are tithing, honouring God with their substance and planting seeds of faith, do not live in fear of want or unemployment. They know their Heavenly Father wants to bless them so they pour their gifts at his feet with prayer, love, expectancy and obedience, and find that their faith is rewarded.

Jesus once watched as the worshippers gave their offerings. He wasn't moved by the plenty some cast into the bowl because he looked at their hearts. When the poor widow threw in her mite he saw what it cost: it was her everything. I wonder if she was embarrassed to give so small a sum? The Lord understands the faith in which all gifts are given.

Sometimes those with persistent problems, sickness or other suffering in their homes will bring a thank offering as an evidence of their faith that God will step in and meet their needs. Giving is a tangible way of expressing faith.

New members are introduced to tithing by the correspondence course which is automatically sent to all converts. The lessons are reinforced by example in the cell groups and through the testimonies and teaching heard in the meetings. Envelopes are provided for those who intend to tithe, printed across the top with Malachi 3:10, a sure encouragement to all givers. One eighth of the church's income is from thank offerings, a half through tithing, and the rest is from other gifts and offerings for particular needs. Yonggi Cho makes no secret of the fact that his church is rich. The people give fifteen million dollars a year, and that figure is constantly increasing.

Once preaching about the blessings of giving he said, 'One thing I cannot be is poor. More than once I have tried to give away everything, my car, my home; but God gives it all back in greater and greater measure. Now I have stopped trying. God is so good that he wants to bless us.'

What he has proved true so have thousands and thousands of his congregation: 'You can't beat God at giving. You can shovel it out, but God will shovel it back, and he has got a bigger shovel!'

That there may be food in my house

There is certainly an abundance of food in Full Gospel Central Church. Multitudes are feasting on a full spiritual diet, day by day growing in the truth of God's word and becoming mighty warriors in Korea and further afield as their vision spreads. Their abundance is not only spiritual food for the people have natural food enough and to spare; surely God has prospered his people.

As a direct result of their generous giving, there is food in the house of God which promotes the growth of the church. The people give sacrificially, and not only out of their abundance. They do not come saying, 'Lord, if you bless me then I will give.' Quite the opposite. They first bless God, and he turns around with a double portion for them.

And I will open the windows of heaven for you

To walk about among the people or to be present at one of their meetings, is evidence enough that God has opened up the windows of heaven and is pouring down an overflowing blessing upon his people. He is rebuking the devourer for them. The land is enjoying good weather and fine crops; year by year their production improves. Government statistics say that there are now twenty-two per cent active Christians and the church projects that by 1990 seventy per cent will be Christian. As the blessing that God continues to pour out affects the life of Korea and spreads throughout the world, surely all the nations will call Korea blessed. The curse of robbing God has been removed from the land. The people obey the scripture and bring their full tithes into the storehouse, so God is fulfilling his promise. He has opened the windows of heaven upon them and is pouring down an overflowing blessing.

3. POWER THROUGH THE HOLY SPIRIT

The senior partner

I had never more clearly seen how the church is an extension of heaven upon earth, until I went to Seoul. There I met Jesus revealed in people living the heaven lifestyle with the beauty of God's power among them, made gloriously possible because he had sent the Holy Spirit. Where the Holy Spirit is honoured and loved he permeates every area, so making the church an extension of heaven; just like its outer office! The differentiating factor between a secular organisation and the church is the Spirit. The church devoid of the Spirit is just an organisation. His presence tinges all its activities with the supernatural, lifting it out of all worldly comparisons and endorsing its heavenly claim.

Where the Spirit of God moves powerfully he is moving in people powerfully, not floating about in the air. He himself is the dynamic for his church, which he channels through people.

Many Christians have a sense of inadequacy which leads them constantly to seek the Spirit; when the answer lays in moving out in faith, and believing in the power of God that is within them.

Yonggi Cho is such a positive person that in a few sentences he can turn his people from inward ways of thinking, to praising God. As they praise him for what they do have they are released to progressively experience the power of the Spirit upon their lives.

Power to plan

We all wish we knew what lay ahead. How simple it would be in business or government if the coming years yielded up their secrets. Planning for the future would be no problem.

The church is the only organisation on earth which has the glorious facility of understanding and knowing the future, which God holds in his hands. With precision he guides us upon his chosen path, shedding understanding and revelation at the right time so that we are not caught unawares. We can prepare safely for the future.

Yonggi Cho's partnership with the Holy Spirit is such a vital, secure relationship that where the Spirit leads him, he is happy to go. All big organisations need projected growth rates, funds and facilities for future expansion. Cho says, 'The Holy Spirit is the senior partner and I am the junior.' As the senior partner knows exactly what the future holds, and the junior partner is ready to implement all his instructions, success is assured. Cho's partnership gives him courage to spell out his plans and stimulates him to work efficiently, producing the framework through which the Holy Spirit's power can flow. Securely Cho can go ahead and dig up the car park to extend the main auditorium, planning and preparing for the huge influx he expects by 1984, all because his projected growth rate has been given by the senior partner in God's business on earth.

God's ultimate plan for his church soon comes clear with a long hard look at Calvary. Jesus lived on earth in the mighty power of the Holy Spirit, bringing heaven down upon our sin-sick world. Then in his spotless untarnished body he gathered up all the sin and foul wickedness that humanity had ever known and carried it away to the depths of hell. Whilst bearing that intolerable burden, with arms outstretched to the whole world, the eyes of our Lord Jesus pierced through millenia to see a host which no man could number dressed in pure garments, washed in the blood of the Lamb. Looking from his vantage point he anticipated the day when he would stand in the midst of that enormous congregation and praise God with his brothers. Therefore, after he had borne away the sin of the world, straight from the God-forsaken dying experience of Calvary, he ascended to the right hand of God the Father, and poured out the Holy Spirit so that the vision of his own heart should come into being: no longer one solitary body filled with the Spirit, but now a body as vast as the ends of the earth, reaching to every nation bringing glory and honour to God.

Full Gospel Central Church have stood with Jesus, satiated their spirits with the sight and found themselves fired by the joy that was set before Christ as he hung upon the cross, their heart beat quickened by his. He died so that no one need perish; the work he accomplished at Calvary paid the debt for everyone, so immense was his vision.

In Central Church the Holy Spirit's power is a reality, not just a Christian teaching. He is the deciding factor: 'If God is for us, who is against us?'[3] If the Lord says go they are ready and raring. Having no other plans besides the direction of the Holy Spirit, they are always in the majority with him whatever the opposition.

Power to witness

The best way to demonstrate the power of electricity is to put it to use. In the same way the Holy Spirit's power is seen through what he accomplishes in his church.

Any visitor to Full Gospel Central Church is first overwhelmed by its size; the impact nearly bowls one over. What a glorious demonstration of the work of the Spirit. This is what he can do through ordinary believers. Boldness was one of the main characteristics when the Holy Spirit fell upon the first Christians in the Acts of the Apostles. They went everywhere boldly declaring the Word of God. It's the same in Seoul where fearlessly men and women baptised in the Holy Spirit preach the Word with bold audacity wherever the Spirit leads. Jesus instructed his disciples to wait until they received the baptism in the Holy Spirit, when they would have power to be witnesses.

The fruit of the Spirit transforms lives, revolutionising them and creating a devastating testimony. The world sits up and takes notice; they are baffled when adulterers return home to become responsible husbands and fathers or where the grip of gambling is broken. A new life is indisputable and shouts to an unbelieving world that in God there is power to change, stirring hope and faith in those who long to be different.

Power to teach

By the power of the Holy Spirit the people are taught, exhorted, encouraged, counselled and comforted. The precious Spirit has promised all these provisions and many more. The simplicity with which the Word of God is approached and believed brings power among his people. 'The Holy Spirit will lead you into all truth. He will teach you all things' (John 16:13). These simple hearted believers expect him to do it.

As I moved among the people in Central Church I had the impression that in the West we are often far too clever, substituting many man-made alternatives for the power of the Holy Spirit.

None of the church's teaching programmes approach scripture in a carnal analytical fashion but only from the premise that it is God's word and therefore the Holy Spirit is happy to be their teacher. Yonggi Cho expresses his disappointment with so many bible schools which give information about God or, even worse, fill the heads of the students with masses of unbelieving information with which to attack the scripture. He strongly advises all his young people who are looking for further training to go only to bible institutes where they are taught to know God, not just taught about him; to study the bible rather than spend years learning about the bible. With that emphasis the scripture is taught and the Spirit honoured.

Power to heal

The testimonies to healing and miracles are endless in Central Church. Frequently, in the large public meetings, Yonggi Cho exercises the word of knowledge, and will say, for instance, 'All those here with a stiff neck stand up.' By mentioning particular complaints and ailments, faith is stimulated in those suffering who then rise to their feet claiming their healing from Jesus. Cho will pray for them. Others are healed spontaneously during the worship times. On Sundays, between the meetings, the pastors and the section heads will be at their desks praying for one after another with problems or sicknesses. A queue forms as they wait to have hands laid upon them to receive their healing or deliverance.

The pastors themselves are the busiest men, running here and there to pray with people in their times of trouble. They conduct funerals, have teaching sessions with new converts, discuss home cells but whatever their timetable, when a crisis occurs they are ready to abandon their programme and respond to the emergency.

One day Mr Chung Kab Whai, an owner of a bakery, was admitted to St. Pasta's Hospital in Seoul. The family called the pastor, who learned that Mr Chung had a gallstone and was to have an operation the following day.

As Pastor Lee prayed, God was saying in his heart that

the man didn't need an operation, that he was healed. Feeling a little nervous, he prayed again, but he was not brave enough to tell the man that he was now well. After praying a third time, he felt convinced so turning to him he commanded his healing, but still hadn't got the courage to say, 'You might as well go home; you are all right.' Compromising he said, 'Why don't you postpone your operation? You certainly won't die if you wait for one more day. Pray, and ask them to give you another X-ray.' Together they agreed that that was the best plan. After praying, hugging and crying together Pastor Lee left.

He was unable to visit the hospital for another two days, and then found Mr Chung Kab Whai had already been discharged. Quickly he went to his home to find out what had happened. When they had X-rayed him there was no sign of the gall-stone. Exactly as God had told Pastor Lee, he was healed.

People in Central Church expect to be healthy and healed. Sickness is regarded as a curse that should be prayed about and resisted in the name of Jesus. During pastoral visiting many receive healing, and it is part of the general life of the cell groups. Those with problems share them with trusted leaders. Only those with authority to do so are permitted to lay hands upon the believers, a privilege given when their wisdom and maturity is approved.

Qualified by the spirit

'Did you receive the Spirit when you believed?'[4] That is a very relevant question in Central Church, as no one can function in any position of leadership unless they have experienced the baptism in the Holy Spirit and, more than that, walk in his fulness day by day. The power supply through the Holy Spirit would soon dry up unless the individual church members are continuously refreshed in his presence. Daily the ministers gather to worship the Lord, seeking a fresh infilling of his Spirit to be their enabling, recognising that to trust man's wisdom is like leaning on a broken stick.

Because this attitude is so deeply embedded in the leadership it comes out in the teaching to the whole church at every level. Day by day the pastoral staff are instructing groups and classes, and counselling individuals. The pastors recognise it is only the power of the Holy Spirit which can motivate the church and enthuse them to fulful the demanding responsibility that is upon them in these days. The effort required to whip up enthusiasm or cajole half-alive believers to witness and stand firm for the gospel is too much, but if they are empowered by the Spirit no one will be able to hold them down.

All new believers are encouraged to be baptised in the Holy Spirit. Some receive the gift as soon as they are born again, some through counselling by their pastors or in their home cells and yet others go to Prayer Mountain, where they fast and pray until God pours his Spirit upon them. The baptism in the Holy Spirit is not taught as something special for a few believers, but as a necessity for all. He is the power by which they witness.

As the Spirit of God falls upon believers, they are encouraged to speak in tongues, and to move on from there to receive other gifts.

In the main gatherings many praise God in other tongues, but the size of the meeting inhibits the ministry of individual gifts from the body of believers. Thus whatever gifts are manifested come from those on the platform. But at smaller meetings, and in the home cells, the gifts of the Holy Spirit are used. Some prophesy and give messages in tongues with interpretation, but the main emphasis is on faith, miracles, healings and the word of knowledge, rather than the vocal gifts.

Yonggi Cho has a remarkably open attitude to any manifestation of the Holy Spirit. He is not one to stand on the sidelines judging and criticising the experience of others, saying, 'That's not the way we do it.' He tells a story which shows his childlike approach of an occasion when the Spirit fell upon many people causing them to shake. It was something he had never experienced himself so when he got back to his room he shut the door and said to the Spirit, 'I am here now, let me shake.' And very amusingly, he says, the Spirit fell upon him and he shook from top to bottom, and thoroughly enjoyed it!

On a recent visit to Australia, where the people were dancing in the Spirit he anticipated getting liberated in that manifestation also.

I never saw any disorder at Central Church. They were very free in praying, shouting, singing with their hands raised and clapping, but always controlled by the Spirit. Obviously among such huge crowds there will be those who have got demonic problems, but on the occasions when I witnessed them those in authority quickly took charge. The devil would love to create confusion and so discredit the genuine. Evil manifestations are no cause for the church to inhibit or restrict the wholehearted seeking of the Holy Spirit, or his true manifestations.

4. POWER TO EVANGELISE

God knows evangelism is only possible by his power. The Spirit of God is right there providing his dynamic ability to witness, endorsing the activity of those zealous believers co-operating with his purposes to establish the kingdom. Power to evangelise flows straight from his throne.

Alongside the church buildings at Yoido, there is a vast plaza where for five evenings in August 1981 two to three million people gathered to hear the Gospel. Yonggi Cho and other preachers co-operated with the churches of nineteen denominations in this huge venture, probably it was the largest Christian gathering in history. However, special evangelistic meetings are not the normal means of growth for Full Gospel Central Church, where the emphasis is on personal witness, which they do with an expectation that the word will be received and the person will turn to the Lord. The majority make their commitment to Christ in one of the main gatherings of the church, when Yonggi Cho challenges people to stand in response to the claim of Christ upon their lives.

The evangelistic arm of the church reaches wherever there are people. Some visit prisons and hospitals, others stand in the streets giving out tracts and newspapers, while those burdened to take the word of God to the army, where all Korean young men do a period of training, visit their camps. Many with specialist concerns are formed into vital evangelising fellowships within the framework of the church so that their activity builds the church rather than creating para-church organisations.

The university students have their own outreach called The Christian Ambassador Mission which began early in 1981 has already formed one hundred prayer groups in colleges in and around Seoul. Student leaders gather the young people together for bible study, and many have been saved. The Mission is still in its infancy, yet they plan to expand it into many more colleges and institutions.

The next step for many students is to join the Graduates Fellowship, which is geared to utilise the abilities of these young people in their new fields of work and responsibility.

The fine new World Mission Building, accommodating all the evangelistic and mission activities of the church is an expression of the big heart for evangelism in Central Church, which is symbolised by the relief map of the world in the entrance.

Various departments and organisations are at present moving their offices into the new building from the old one which is to become an education centre.

The Church Growth International (C.G.I.) Department is to take up residence on the eleventh floor in the new building. From there they will keep in touch with the activities of growing churches worldwide and organise church growth seminars. Since its inception C.G.I. has held one hundred seminars in which 40,000 foreign pastors and lay-leaders have been taught the principles of church growth.

World of Faith Magazine has presented the church at Yoido to the world through its faith building articles describing what God has done. As the Spirit of God moves in other countries large churches are beginning to emerge and to encourage faith and share the joy of what God is doing worldwide, a new magazine will be published from Spring 1982 called 'Church Growth Ministries International'.

It is exceptionally difficult to separate evangelism at home and mission work abroad. It seems inevitable that zeal for evangelism which reaches into every area of life at home is eventually going to find expression spreading its wings further and further abroad.

By all means to reach some

Modern Korea offers the opportunity of radio and television for evangelism and Yonggi Cho hasn't been slow to take up the challenge. Since 1966 when he began with a weekly five minute thought his radio ministry has extended to weekly sermons now relayed from eight stations touching the whole country. Television presented the next golden opportunity and since 1980 weekly programmes have been beamed into four districts of Korea. The expert television and mass media department, a truly competent and professional group in the church, is already working on expanding these to the larger population areas. There are massive opportunities through this ministry. At one viewing of a television programme or at the switch of a radio knob millions can be reached with the gospel. This powerful medium is being exploited to the full. Radio programmes are now beamed into Russia and in Mandarin to the whole of China.

To us it may sound unnecessary for a nation like Korea to spend its time and money evangelising the United States, where the range of Christian television broadcasts is mesmerizing; one would wonder why Full Gospel Central Church would want to join with such competition.

In 1981 Dr Cho was invited to speak at a religious inaugural event for President Reagan in Washington D.C. He says that during that time God challenged him to put time, money and effort into presenting the gospel to the United States to repay the debt for their involvement in saving his nation from the Communists and for bringing the gospel to Korea almost one hundred years ago.

In response, hour long programmes of the Korean Services at Central Church are broadcast in Los Angeles, and New York, besides radio programmes in Korean to New York, Dallas, Houston and Washington D.C. intended for the very large Korean immigrant population in those cities.

And the printed page

If I hadn't seen it with my own eyes I would find it hard to believe that one church could produce so many newspapers and magazines, all of such excellent quality. Besides the World of Faith magazine mentioned earlier there is the 'Shinangge Magazine', a 148-page monthly that has grown and grown in circulation to 54,000 copies and is sold on secular book stalls as well as to subscribers. It is a powerful evangelistic tool with first class testimonies of salvation and healing, encouraging faith in believers and helping non-Christians to find Christ.

The Yongsan Publishing Company, part of the church's organisation produces a children's magazine 'Beautiful Star' for the pre-teen age group again sold on secular book stalls. Then there is the church newspaper, 'Full Gospel News', which goes out free to as many people as want it. Yongsan, besides publishing Dr Yonggi Cho's books and many others written by the staff, also produces cassette ministry tapes in English and Korean. The quantity of evangelistic tapes, books and literature that pour from the various ministries in Full Gospel Central Church is overwhelming. One thing they all have in common is their good quality and reasonable price.

Over the past years Japan has been the centre for the church's evangelistic activities. Dr Cho has a vision of evangelising ten million Japanese during the 1980s and to bring this dream into reality he visits Japan on a monthly basis, taking pastors' and leaders' conferences all over the land and encouraging the local Christians to believe for growth and to evangelise. To back up this ministry Yongsan is now launching out into a Japanese version of 'Shinangge Magazine', and already there are weekly television broadcasts of the Sunday services in north and south Japan. Translated into Japanese they are reaching up to sixty million each week.

Little Korea cannot rest while alongside is the giant communist China. From her meagre resources she longs to take the gospel to the nation with the largest population on the face of the earth. Because of economic strictures in Korea unlimited quantities of foreign exchange may not be exported, but to evangelise a country as huge as China calls for endless supplies of money.

However, besides being a very godly man, Cho is also very shrewd. I had to smile when he said, 'If we evangelise ten million Japanese we can then use Yen, an unrestricted currency, to evangelise 700 million Chinese.' The world and all that's in it belongs to the Lord. Cho, like a good businessman, makes forward financial planning for his next move! Their motivation to evangelise knows no bounds; a country as huge as China does not daunt little Korea; for they believe in God they have resources to meet all the world's needs.

And into all the world

The church has its own missionary association and so far has sent out ninety-two missionaries who have built eighty-two churches in sixty different countries scattered around the world, the majority among Korean communities. They have also established bible schools, one in Berlin, another in Los Angeles, a third in Kobe, Japan, and one each in New York and Chicago, where they train Korean missionary candidates. Each year in Seoul the Missions Convention, where the missionaries are presented to the people and their worldwide activities shared, continues to get larger. By 1984 they plan to have 400 missionaries, and already one married couple have come to Wimbledon in England. When speaking of Central Church's missionary programme Mr Jongkyu Shim said, 'No power on earth can deter the mighty advance of the gospel when the

Holy Spirit is permitted to equip and to empower his people for evangelism."[5]

Let the little ones come unto me

One of the most remarkable spheres of evangelism is to the children of Seoul. In May 1981 there were 45,261 gathered together in children's cell groups, and by now that number will be far greater. These little ones meet on Saturday afternoons in the homes of teachers who use lesson material provided by the church. The majority of the children are not yet converted, one teacher estimated that seventy per cent of her group were non-Christians.

The Christian children bring their friends, because from their youngest years they are being trained to be good evangelists. Often a child coming to the Lord means that the door is open into the home. Many parents and whole families have found Christ through this vigorous evangelistic work.

Industrial evangelism

Many of the teenagers, once they leave school, are employed in one of the thousands of Seoul's small manufacturing industries, where they receive pitiably small salaries. The Industrial Evangelism Department is now reaching out to contact young people in an area where many of these factories are located. The church has leased a building where young workers can have their cell meetings, bible study and prayer times, as well as learning many practical skills, and some receive help to complete their formal education. Leaders among them who work in the factories reach out to the young people encouraging them to turn to Christ. Although at first some of the factory owners are very hesitant about this kind of influence among their workers, their fears have been completely allayed by the example of those who have turned to Christ. When they see how hard working and responsible these young people have become the opposition evaporates.

The Gideon Fellowship

To add to the special ministry of Industrial Evangelism the Gideon Fellowship aims to reach eight million men and women employed in offices and factories throughout Korea. Strategic evangelism aimed at specific areas of the community is very productive and this is the strength of the Gideon Fellowship. With the purpose of evangelising the factories they contact Christians and bring them together to pray and witness in their local work place. The power and effectiveness of their evangelism stems from its collective nature. They encourage one another and once a month share a day together in prayer and fasting for the work.

Some pastors assist them by arranging meetings and daily, through literature and talking with people, many are converted. Frequently the best way of witnessing is to invite the contact to Central Church because it is such a fantastic attraction that it isn't too difficult to get them there, even if they come only out of curiosity to see the largest church in the world.

What comes first, the chicken or the egg?

Evangelism is part of the power of Full Gospel Central Church but you might legitimately ask, 'How can we get people motivated to evangelise in the dedicated fashion that they do in Seoul? What comes first? Do people just begin to witness and trust the power of the Spirit to direct them?' In the church the ministry encourages every believer, even the newest convert, to be an effective, vital witness. It is the ethos of the church, and becomes the impetus with which they begin their Christian lives. Like all of us, as they step out into the spiritual battle to rescue people from the kingdom of darkness, they recognise their own pitiable resources and cry for the power of the Spirit upon their lives, with the command of scripture, 'to go' ringing in their ears.

Part of the motivation is the sheer weight of numbers. It is so much easier to be bold when you are one of a big crowd. In fact not to be a witness would make you the odd one out. It doesn't in any way devalue the witness or its results, but it is just easier to speak of Christ to non-Christians when in the company of others doing the same thing. There is power in numbers.

A repeated theme in all the praying in Korea is that God would cause them to become a completely Christian nation. They believe that the remarkable revival will continue until a large majority have become born again believers. The oustanding success of the evangelistic outreach of the church is sufficient encouragement for everyone to become wholeheartedly involved, in what is to them, a realisable goal.

SIX

Words that build

When Pastor Cho stands up to preach he brings a message which is simple yet profound, milk as well as meat, to a congregation spread out before him representing the whole gamut of Christian experience from new babes through to wise old saints, plus a good sprinkling of those seeking the Lord.

The congregation at Yoido are people who have come to their local church, not floating visitors attending a special meeting. Week by week after long bus journeys, despite the discomfort and crush, they fill the buildings without fail. Understandably you might ask what is the attraction? It must be something unusual to draw such gatherings and produce so many conversions.

Out of the seven services each Sunday Pastor Cho preaches at four. Whatever his programme for the week he plans to be in Seoul for the maximum number of Sundays in a year. It is his weekly opportunity to be among his people. He belongs to them, despite his ever-increasing responsibilities overseas, and they belong to him. The bond is strongly forged by his dependable presence. The variety of other ministry in the Church is diverse and readily available, but Pastor Cho's appearance and ministry Sunday by Sunday draws the vast conglomeration of organisations, cells and activities together and declares, 'we are one.' He unifies the whole work. The people come to hear Yonggi Cho; he is loved, respected and honoured. They know the miracle of Full Gospel Central Church would never have been except for him.

He is not a gimmick preacher or charismatic in a worldly way. The bible is his text book and the simple gospel his message. With childlike simplicity he declares that the blood of Jesus is our only answer to sin. Nothing is impossible to God; by his stripes we were healed. Seek first the kingdom of God and all these things shall be added unto you. All things? Yes, everything. Everything that you need it is your heavenly father's delight to supply.

As the stream of people move up the stairs into the main auditorium a text, with letters two feet high is seen across the wall: 'Beloved I pray that in all respects you may prosper and be in good health, just as your soul prospers.' (3 John v. 2.) The three-fold blessings wrapped up in this verse are a familiar chord in Yonggi Cho's preaching by which he encourages the people that God is there to bless them. Korean life does not offer a selection of options, and many of his congregation would have come to God as their only hope.

Society is chequered with painful problems all of which are represented in the crowd walking up the stairs. Medical care is phenomenally expensive and often sophisticated treatments are only available to those with plenty of money. Unfortunately immorality in society brings many heart-broken wives to the church seeking comfort. Others come depressed, considering themselves useless. Yonggi Cho feels all these needs among the people as if they were his own. He aches for those who come unworthy, unloved, rejected, or as hopeless failures. He says it is not his job as a preacher of the Good News of Jesus Christ to lay yet more condemnation and blame upon them, but to bring a message of light and hope to lift them out of their state. 'God will bless you in your spirit and soul, in your family and business, favouring you with the blessing of good health' Yonggi Cho preaches.

Positive thinking

Everything about Pastor Cho is positive, exhortative and encouraging and as he preaches he produces these beautiful qualities in the people. Everything he says is simple and very exact, provoking the congregation to expect God to bless them. He lives in the blessing of God himself and delights to shed it upon them. Positive thinking keeps the door open for continual blessing.

Some think that any benefits derived from positive thinking are only concocted by self-effort, but Cho's teaching is rooted in the scripture which says, 'Seek first the kingdom of God and all these things shall be added unto you.'[1] He puts the emphasis in the right place and again and again insists that this is where the power lies: if his people will first seek God they will inherit his promises.

Typically, he would point out the tragedy of negative attitudes saying, 'If you worry about failure you will fail; if you worry about being fearful you will fear.' He would charge his people not to think negatively, and plainly warn where it would lead them, instructing them to turn and engage their minds in the truth of God's Word. 'Cast all your anxieties upon him because he cares for you.'[2] He would say, 'Rejoice! God has not given you a spirit of fear[3] so do not allow your mind to dwell upon those things which are fearful.'

Possibility thinking

Closely connected with positive thinking is possibility thinking, and this isn't 'pie in the sky' dreaming but a genuine expression of the extravagant faith that is in Pastor Cho. 'All things are possible to God and all things are possible to those who believe.'[4] He encourages his people to open their hearts to grasp hold of possibilities in God, to pray about them and live in the reality of their fulfilment.

The purpose of Pastor Cho's preaching is not primarily to provide teaching or information but rather to bring his people into experience. He introduces the Word of God to them in such a way that it is like currency, to be used. God has said it, act upon it; it is valid and it will pay off.

Frequently he refers to visions and dreams. In his book 'The Fourth Dimension' he vividly describes this way of faith. It is so much part of him that his preaching motivates his people to have visions and dreams also. He says, 'Look again into the Word of God and see the vast extent of promises and possibilities open to those who believe.'

The setting of goals is vitally linked to bringing visions and dreams from incubation to birth. These goals are realistic, forged in the presence of God and then adhered to and worked out in the fear of the Lord. By this process visions and dreams are possessed, to become realities.

The people call him 'Pastor' Cho, but it is his apostolic and prophetic ministry which has carried a community of people into the place where they possess visions and dreams with him. By thinking, planning, talking and teaching growth Pastor Cho has successfully engaged his members' hearts in a united effort to evangelise. They are enthusiastic for growth. Like the early church they cannot keep quiet; their personal salvation is not an end in itself but rather an opportunity to see someone else saved. Their hearts rejoice that Jesus is glorified by much fruit.

Local and mature

In Full Gospel Central Church the members' day to day needs are met. Surprisingly Cho keeps abreast with the uppermost questions which trouble them and in his own inimitable way applies the Word of God to their immediate problems. Many have come from a background of Shamanism, a type of spirit worship, a conglomeration of occult practices and spiritism. Plainly he points out the error of such ways and brings them lovingly into maturity, showing them that there is freedom in Christ. Without hard condemnation for those in such darkness he cuts them from their old bondages, binding them strongly together in the Word of God so that they are not a collection of individual church goers but a corporate company.

Released people can minister

Yonggi Cho's ministry brings release; he builds confidence in those who feel uneducated or unworthy, by showing that they are more than conquerors in Christ.[5] He lifts the unbearable weight of uselessness and failure from the shoulders of his hearers, especially ministering to women, who naturally have a down-trodden place in society. In Christ all are accepted and made useful by the Holy Spirit. His ministry has produced an army of workmen, motivated and encouraged to attempt anything. They are given responsibility where the successful ones are recognised, brought into leadership, and so the work grows. A released people grow mature, daily exercised in the spiritual activities that God has given them to do. The church was never intended to sit back and watch one overworked man at the front. Although he is the centre of the work, it is built so that if he were to go it would not collapse. All the available diverse gift and ability of the whole body is made usable.

'Rhema' for food

'Let me share a "rhema" the Lord has given me today.' I took out my bible and Pastor Lee shared with me the special word the Lord had given him that morning. Like the boy with the five loaves and two fishes, he opened up his valued supplies to feed us all.

Dr Cho's ministry encourages each person to reach beyond just bible reading, to receiving a 'rhema', a word from God specially for the day, which will feed them and make them grow. Like having a good meal set before us rather than walking round the supermarket seeing all the food stacked on the shelves, a 'rhema' is there ready to be eaten, digested and enjoyed. By the daily 'rhema' from the Word of God his people grow mature because they experience communion with God instead of only gaining knowledge.

A world-wide vision

'Go into all the world and preach the gospel to every creature',[6] written in Korean and English is also in two-foot high letters on the walls of the auditorium. Never a meeting goes by without prayer being offered for the church worldwide. Mission is at the very heart of the church. It is impossible for Yonggi Cho to preach a small gospel; his heart is as big as Jesus'.

Strangely it is the burden for the nations which stimulates building the church in Korea. As their own land becomes more and more Christian they sense a responsibility to share what God has given them with the whole world. They believe that a really huge church is a valid expression of the bigness of the power that is in Jesus. The buoyant faith of the church in tiny Korea is enough to spur them to take the world on single-handed. They have such a big view of God and his ability and power through them.

As Yonggi Cho provokes the people to pray and give for world mission one senses his deep gratitude and thanks to God for all that he has done in their little land. They express a sense of genuine debt to the whole world. There is an urgency in their hearts for world evangelism. No one could be in the church for long before feeling their own responsibility to the world. Many young people and families are preparing themselves to serve God overseas as Yonggi Cho persistently presents the need and challenge before them. His ministry is producing a large contingent of missionaries who are motivated to work while there is still the opportunity. Many doors are shut and others contested, but with all their heart and strength they are involved in the fight to see the nations of the world brought under the rule of the King of Kings.

Education in depth

Week by week thousands are added to the church, mainly gathered in during the time when Yonggi Cho is preaching. To build these new converts in the fundamentals of the faith there are special classes arranged. Others who wish to have a closer working knowledge of the Word of God with perhaps a view to becoming housegroup leaders or bible teachers, can attend the Laymen's Bible School which offers a fourteen week course. The students cover a survey of the entire bible. After graduating they are qualified to enter the Laymen's Bible College where a six-month course is offered in twenty topics and systematic bible theology. At every level of Christian life there is opportunity for learning, growing and maturing. Whether the lesson is for a class of toddlers or for research students, it is shot through and coloured by Yonggi Cho's own childlike approach to the Word of God. Fanciful notions of what the scripture might mean would find no place in any of the teaching establishments of Full Gospel Central Church. Their message is founded on words that build.

SEVEN

The sign

When God gives a sign it demands our attention, like a signal, 'Stand up! Take note! Look!' It declares a truth, or unfolds a new aspect of his will presenting a key to further realms of spiritual revelation and experience.

The bible says, 'In the last days . . . I will show wonders in the heaven above and signs on the earth beneath.'[1] What a privilege to be given signs; they are not shown to all, so let us be sensitive enough to recognise them. In this age of reason we could easily brush aside God's voice with rational explanations and prove to be no better than the Scribes and Pharisees of Jesus' day.

Signs are gifts of grace, spiritual pointers given at crucial times as when reaching a turning point, but they are never understood by the idly curious. They are interpreted only to sincere seeking hearts. As we take time to observe what God is doing he will enlighten our spirits. We are not engaged in a spiritual guessing game; we are his friends and he wants to show us what he is doing. What folly if we fail to look and understand.

The bible tells of many different kinds of signs, each a demonstration of power and each bringing glory to Jesus. At the wedding in Cana when Jesus did his first miracle it says the occasion 'manifested his glory; and his disciples believed in him.'[2] Glory seems to be always linked with signs.

Angelic hosts declared to the frightened shepherds in Bethlehem that they would find a babe wrapped in swaddling clothes and lying in a manger: a very ordinary event, a baby like any other of his age, but the angels said, 'This will be a sign for you.'[3] Unobtrusively God slipped into the world in human flesh – the most profound happening of all times, but announced to so few. In heaven the angels couldn't keep quiet but the earth lay silent and unaware of the mighty sign in her midst. Only the shepherds, a privileged audience of heaven's rejoicing, caught the vision and filled with wonder and awe they joined their voices with the angels' praise. The sign brought glory to Jesus. Although phenomenally important, it seems that God is economical in advertising such events. Our Saviour came in obscurity and apparent weakness, unknown except to the shepherds and, perhaps, to the shaking powers of darkness.

We live in the days when the bible says signs will be more frequent; even the evil one will increasingly work his deceiving signs and wonders to create confusion, deluding and leading many astray by his display of obvious supernatural power. In contrast every genuine sign of God commands attention in such a way that we know it is God and not manufactured by men.

A modern day sign

Our contemporary world has shrunk. The daily news confronts us with trans-world trouble; a train crash in Peru, a fire in Australia, a famine in Russia, all clamour for concern and interest. Our knowledgeable children bandy about names almost too difficult to read of once-remote places on a map. Globetrotting holiday plans are made by London bus drivers who in the past never expected to venture further than Southend Pier. To a Welsh hill farmer the idea of an annual break was once as foreign to him as Gruyere cheese; to stand and stare was sheer delight, relaxation enough. But now we run to and fro, worn out by holidays. Photographs keep our memories alive, bringing back those distant places into our living rooms.

Our restless age has produced a unique climate for worldwide pronouncements. Today, if Jesus was born in Bethlehem the shepherds could ring the news network and it could be on our television screens before the day was out. But would it? Certainly any catastrophe is guaranteed rapid coverage in the media and the potential is there to report any happening that is considered news. But what is news? Like quiet revolutions, spiritual revivals in many lands go unheeded, dramatic things can happen without anyone wanting to know.

Our minds have been so battered by horrific events that unconsciously our reactions have become anaesthetised. We need to be aware that the same dulling effect could also permeate our spiritual reactions. If God intervened would we be capable of seeing it or has the spirit of the age produced a cloying veil over our eyes? It is dangerous. What if we were discovered to be as blind as the inn-keeper in Bethlehem on that momentous night?

Are we blind, or can we perceive that God is doing signs in the earth today for us to heed? Pastor Cho conceives of a church of half a million, sets goals, commissions workers, just as a civil engineer plans a new town. News? Surely it is to us, but more than news for those with their eyes focused upon another Kingdom. Could it be at a time such as this when the world is on our doorstep that God has raised up a sign for all the nations?

Something unique has happened in Seoul. Is this a modern day sign? For years Central Church with its huge ever-growing congregation has been unnoticed. Like a great balloon, it expanded quietly till it was so vast that it could no longer remain hidden. God has done a new thing. Never before has there been such a church. Now the world is taking notice; here is a city set on a hill that cannot be hidden.

The sign speaks

In the hills of Nagaland, North East India, revivals have taken place with many thousands turning to Christ. Miracles and outstanding manifestations of the Spirit are numerous as the animist tribes are confronted with the living Christ. An estimated seventy per cent of the population is now Christian, the majority having been swept into the Kingdom during the past twenty years. Nagaland is possibly the most Christian place on the face of the earth, but that doesn't make it a sign.

Full Gospel Central Church with its hundreds of thousands is unique, possessing identity, commitment and pastoral care of such gigantic proportions that it previously would never have been thought possible. As one unified congregation they collectively speak to us as a sign. It is a miraculous visual aid, declaring the mighty power of God over all the powers of the evil one. In the face of persecutions, wars, and other religions the Lord Jesus Christ is building his Church. It proclaims that God has mercy on whom he will have mercy. Korea is becoming a nation of first generation Christians as God pours out his Spirit.

Here is victory over Satan's domain: the strong man is being robbed of his goods. The power of Jesus knows no limit; what can stand in its way? Surely here is a true manifestation of the glory of God, to be seen by those who have spiritual eyes.

Although we are speaking about a congregation of thousands and thousands, not one convert is added without a battle being fought and won in the heavenly realms. This is not a mass movement of 'rice Christians'. Each soul represents a victory and together they are a glorious triumph.

Haven't we all at some time been filled with wonder when the whole landscape is transformed by a blanket of snow? As we drink in the view it is hard to believe that just individual snow flakes falling thick and fast can create such a change. Thousands and thousands of separate unique snowflakes can turn a scene into a wonderland. Thousands upon thousands of individual new converts are bringing heaven down upon earth.

Satan's kingdom is rapidly slipping from between his fingers – yet he hotly contests each deliverance. Comprehend the magnitude of the overcoming might by which the church is built when this warfare is multiplied a thousandfold! Jesus is glorified by much fruit. How great is the glory brought to his name by this sign.

The sign demonstrates how to build and grow

The sign also spells out the manner in which God wants us to gather his harvest in these last days. It speaks of commitment, relationships and collective responsibility. In Seoul are found a company of people no longer content only to enjoy their individual relationship with God. They are filled with a united zeal and common purpose. Intricately joined to one another, they work to establish the Kingdom of God. With understanding they have grasped the collective nature of the body of Christ. God's army is not an individual but a company of rightly related submitted Christians.

Signs are not for copying, but they do declare intrinsic principles. It may not be right in all places to build mammoth churches but we too can have growing congregations in any locality if we obey the fundamental lessons the sign teaches. Their challenge when fully grasped, demands from us an expectancy for continuous expansion. There is no permission in the Word of God to say, 'I have enough.' The sign displays the determined intention of Jesus who died for the whole world to gather his whole harvest. If we see and understand we should fear to set personal limits.

In some places as church buildings have become full, God has opened the way to establish extra congregations, where the house groups in a certain area find a hall and begin meeting together.

Some years ago God showed us by a vision that our growth pattern was to be like strawberry plants. The mature fruit bearing plant puts out a runner and grows another plant, which is sustained until that too becomes fruit bearing. For certain cities and dense population areas nothing other than a huge congregation is adequate to publicise the authority of our God over all contrary claims to power. The variety of ways in which we can grow is endless. Rather than just discussing their pros and cons let's grow!

Signs divide

The raising of Lazarus, that notable sign, polarised attitudes towards Jesus. We read, 'Many of the Jews therefore, who had come with Mary and had seen what Jesus did, believed in him.' Yet the same event compelled the Chief Priests and Pharisees to say, 'What are we to do? For this man performs many signs. If we let him go on thus, everyone will believe in him . . . so from that day on they took counsel how to put him to death' (John 11:45, 47, 48, 53).

A sign declaring Jesus to be the resurrection and the life prompted the religious leaders of that day to plot his death.

What is the Christian world's response to the sign in Seoul? Wonder, praise, excitement, challenge? Many are excited, encouraged to believe for growth on a scale never dreamed of before. Some, shaken from their complacency question their church government, thinking it might hinder growth. Large numbers demand new ways. Old restrictive structures must give way to a flexible framework through which the Spirit can move and guide his whole body.

We are a cautious people and many will find it difficult to be immediately open-hearted to the extravagant work of God in Korea. As we consider the Church's phenomenal growth, let us steadfastly resist the Pharisaical unbelieving heart which looks for ways of explaining away the work of God. Some argue that the expansion is due to the regimented Korean way of life or is perhaps a demonstration of expertise and organisational prowess. How blind can men be? In Jesus' day the Pharisees asked for a sign so that they could deny it. Here before our eyes we have a demonstration of God's ability to build his Church: not a handful gathered in a cold church building, but something worthy of his great and all-powerful name.

Korea our teacher

Six years ago I had a vision and a prophecy. While we were worshipping the Lord I saw a huge tree. It grew so vast and strong that its branches reached all the way around the world. It seemed to me that the tree was also the Lord Jesus Christ, with his arms reaching to the farthest corners of the earth. His hands went into various nations and picked up people, placing them into other lands at his own bidding. As I watched intently, his hand went to Korea where he lifted up chosen ones and placed them in our land. In the past we have sent missionaries all round the world. The Lord impressed upon me that now he was going to bring to us teachers from distant countries, especially from the Far East.

When I first learned of the work of God in Korea this vision and prophecy was brought again immediately to my mind. Could it be that Full Gospel Central Church is to be our teacher provoking us to faith and vision? God intends to stir hunger in our lethargic spirits, as we look and learn what he is doing.

A provocation to the Christian West

Is the sign of any specific relevance to us in Britain? Where does it touch us most?

Over the past few years our churches have been small and we have adjusted our attitudes to accept that as normal. A congregation of three to four hundred has been regarded as a successful work. Those who managed to gather six to eight hundred had a large church.

Full Gospel Central Church is the local church for hundreds of thousands in Seoul, a city approximately the same size as London although more compact and with easier travelling. There are churches within walking distance for most, but they come from every district for the particular life and ministry that is offered. Despite its size it is a local church, not a city gathering of Christians from other churches. The congregation at Yoido are a faithfully committed group, a true expression of the body of the Lord Jesus Christ in Seoul. This sign proclaims an unlimited size for local churches. Through it, God challenges us to a complete change of attitude about what we consider acceptable. We must begin to think big if we are going to grow big. Our potential for growth is governed by our thinking. Surely the demonstration God has set before us should make us think again.

This is especially relevant to us now, when through the so called 'house church movement' new churches are springing up all over the country. The blessing of God is upon these gatherings and they are growing rapidly. Let us not underestimate the size to which they could grow. 'House-church' is a misnomer: public halls are usually their meeting places. Now as these groups reach the three to four hundred mark old attitudes, if not fully rooted out, could become a stricture upon their further growth.

If British Christians have a national characteristic it is individualism. The desire for personal blessing, and a platform for 'my ministry', has stifled the flow of blessing into the community. The sign speaks corporate blessing. There is a particular endowment of power for the committed group who are intent on sharing their common life in God for the purpose of bringing in his Kingdom. Today many individuals who were previously blessed in the charismatic movement have discovered their need of the corporate life of the body. Their inclusion into many new churches has brought mutual blessing. Through Full Gospel Central Church we gain a glimpse into God's heart of how he longs to save and bring people into the security of his church and bless them together before sending them out.

The sign also teaches us that size requires structure. The simple, adjustable organisation they have evolved has aided the expansion of the work of God and is itself part of the miracle. It is spiritual and efficient in the face of constant change. Certainly, conceived in heaven.

Yonggi Cho's church is a demonstration of how we can 'hold the catch' when God pours out his spirit. In many past revivals the results have been dissipated, but that need not happen again. By careful preparation now our churches can become centres of revival capable of securely building-in each new convert so as to actively extend the body of Christ, which will influence our nation, and change history.

The nothings of this world

'Fancy God favouring a nation like Korea with a deluge of his Holy Spirit.' We are not the only ones to think such a thought. The Koreans themselves, a nation that had almost lost its identity, like pawns in a cruel chess game, wonder at the mercy of God. They seemed to be doomed to failure, frequently expressing an abysmally low value of themselves. But what do we see now? Success and prosperity.

When the ark of the covenant rested for just three months in the house of Obed-edom the bible says, 'The Lord blessed the household of Obed-edom and all that he had' (1 Chron. 13:14). The blessing of God is plainly evident in Korea. Those who were nothing are now an outstanding success: once refugees, they are now exporting businessmen; once scraping around for food, now they have enough and to spare; those who dressed in rags are now well clad. The poor have dwindled away as the blessing of success has spread across the land. The ark of the presence of God has blessed Korea in terms that she understands.

God does not need our western resources or abilities. He will take up those who have reached rock bottom, whether individuals or nations, to demonstrate his power through them. Full Gospel Central Church, growing out of the soil of an 'insignificant' land like Korea shows us again how God delights in the nothings of the world. He has not chosen the wise or the rich, whom he sent away empty.

If we read the sign carefully and take him to understand what God is saying, we too can come to him on the same terms and find he will not send us away.

God's war horse

The conquered and vanquished have now become overcomers, warriors for their God. Their prayer lives have become a demonstration of the militant church. No longer are they on the defensive but vigorously pushing back the powers of darkness in an area of the world where Satan has ruled for too long. Their prayer life is a sign to us: this is how the church is to enter into the sufferings of Christ and through that victory execute his authority on earth.

The following is an account of a vision which the Rev G. Kuhl of Sydney, Australia, received on the last day of his fast at Prayer Mountain, in 1980.

'By the fourteenth day of my fast, God had given me great strength. I felt led by God to go for a walk into villages around Prayer Mountain and as I watched Korean life, God opened my eyes to see a bigger reality.

'I saw China and Russia as a dark continent in a world, ruled over by powerful demon princes who had been there virtually unchallenged for millennia. Then I saw South Korea, like a small beachhead for Holy Spirit warfare in God's spiritual military strategy. On the beachhead of South Korea God had created powerful warriors who were using his most powerful weapon – intercessory prayer. These warriors were holding back the forces of darkness, preventing them from sweeping into South Korea. Satan desperately wants to crush this troublesome little beachhead on his most powerful possession – Asia.

'In the midst of the warriors of South Korea I saw a huge fortress – it gave strength to the warriors. The fortress was Full Gospel Central Church Yoido. Then I understood why God had raised up such a powerful church in this part of the world. It was vitally strategic to God's greater purposes for mankind.

'Then I saw going forth from the praying warriors a stream of fire into the dark continent of Asia. The fire was the Holy Spirit prayer which linked up Christian with Christian in an underground network in Asia. It was so secret that hardly anyone knew of it and certainly not Satan.

'When God's time had fully come I saw God say to this underground network, "Come forth!"

'The network became visible for all to see. The demons shrieked in horror as they saw God's army come forth.

The demons had been secretely ambushed by God's strategy.

'There was a great victory of God.'

Few would dispute that we live in the last days. Jesus is coming soon. We are instructed in many passages of scripture that all the nations shall come to him. What an encouragement it is to see it happening before our eyes. Asia, that great Satanic bastion, must yield. All the nations shall come unto our God. Korea again finds herself to be the beachhead for warfare into Asia, but this time of a different nature.

She has become the harbinger of the message of life. Whereas in the past Britain had the privilege of sending countless missionaries worldwide now Korea has taken up the task. As we see what God is doing may we be provoked to a godly jealousy which stirs the depths of our spirits, bringing us to repentance, and usefulness to aid the worldwide spread of the gospel.

Time is short. In God's mercy he has shown us a great sign. The first one in the New Testament was the babe in the manger, the body of Christ on the earth. In these last days, another sign has been revealed which shows us more clearly what the body of Christ upon earth should be like in our generation.

Yonggi Cho would never consider his church to be perfect. Like everything on our sin-tainted globe there is room for improvement. But there it is, raised up by God for all the world to see, with its flaws and problems given a public viewing. Yet they only serve to emphasise the magnificence of God's handiwork. Look at what he has done, despite the frailty and sinfulness of man. Let your vision and faith rise. Today it is not a baby-sized body we are called to view, but a sign that tells us that his body will fill the whole earth and be completed by all the nations.

EIGHT

God can do it here!

'One has but to know when the proper moment has come and the thread of itself will pass through the needle's eye.' Young Chen in *P'ing Mei*.

Jesus said, 'Lift up your eyes and see how the fields are already white for harvest.'[1] Surely the time is now.

Outwardly it may not appear that we are on the brink of a visitation of the Spirit, but in the experience of Abraham it was only after all natural hope was gone, and he was as good as dead, that God moved miraculously to create life. God has repeated that pattern down the centuries. Time and again, at our point of hopelessness, when all appeared to be lost, when the social and economic scene was black, he stepped in to answer the prayers of his humbled people.

Time is not on our side, but God is. Although wickedness is rampant and the powers of darkness may appear to have the advantage, it is God who holds time in his hand and through his mighty power he can do the work of a thousand years in but a day. Isn't that what we look for? Yes, surely we come with anticipation to our God for a gracious outpouring of his Holy Spirit in these last days, which will bring in the harvest that he has prepared.

The preparation is under way

I am more than ever convinced that now is God's time to move by his Holy Spirit. Everything in the church is pointing to this. The work of God is on tiptoes, expectant and waiting to take hold of something that is really big, but which it does not fully understand.

God's time is now because the signs all point to Jesus coming again soon. The Spirit is active in the body preparing his bride; a clarion voice like that of John the Baptist, the Elijah, is lifted up saying, 'Prepare the way of the Lord.' Talking in his day Jesus said, 'Elijah is coming, and will restore all things' (Matt. 17:11, 12 NASB). The voice of the prophet has gone forth again to the people of God, in our generation, exhorting them to make ready, for the King of Kings is on the way.

The charismatic movement was but part of that preparation ministry of the Spirit of Elijah. It can be likened to John the Baptist's instructions to the disciples to look for Jesus, who would baptise them in the Holy Spirit and with fire. Through the baptism in the Holy Spirit thousands have been brought into a fresh, vital relationship with the Lord.

We were endued with power from on high, which has enriched the life of the church, bringing liberty and a new dimension of prayer. Humble believers have begun learning how to tear down the powers of darkness as a small preparation for the valiant all-out assault which must come upon the hosts of wickedness in our land. Initially our intercessions were random, but as we have learnt more of the strategy of prayer, empowered believers have been systematically undermining the defences of the evil one, though the measure of our successes may not be openly acknowledged yet.

Recently, a school teacher had a significant vision during the few minutes break between classes. The Spirit's presence was suddenly very intense, so he asked the Lord what he wished to say. There before him, he saw a man in a small square room hanging wall paper to cover up the cracking walls. It was a thankless task as fresh cracks were appearing all the time, where the walls were beginning to fall away. The man ran from one crack to another in a makeshift cover-up job. As the school teacher watched, God said, 'The devil is busily running around papering over the cracks of his tottering kingdom. He doesn't want you to know the chaos your onslaught in prayer is causing.' As he looked further he saw that there was only one roll of paper left on the table. The devil is running out of wall paper!

Besides having a devastating prayer ministry, the charismatic Christian has been endued with gifts of the Spirit. These power gifts are making deep inroads into the kingdom of darkness. Prophecy has stirred the people of God to expectancy and belief, so that now they are waiting for the outpouring of God's Spirit. Through this gift, the negative, unbelieving condemning thoughts consistently sown by the evil one are being rooted up.

Those who pray in tongues speak mysteries to God in the Spirit, and who knows what havoc they wreak behind the lines of the kingdom of darkness? Many demons have been cast out as the faith of people has risen. Today in our churches we have healings, words of wisdom and knowledge; we long for more, and especially for the gifts of faith and miracles, to be powerfully released among us. The charismatic movement has brought life to many dry bones, which have come together in a forging of strong joints. The spiritual supply which each possess flows to the benefit of the whole body which is becoming active and healthy and is moving on till it becomes the great army of the Lord.

Restoration

Restoration is the natural progression for people who are walking in the Spirit. As we keep on, God will shed greater and greater light upon the scripture, giving understanding of how he intends to build his church. He will give us clarity so that we know what is important seeing plainly which things should be left behind and which should be incorporated with vigour into the life of the church.

Many churches are like overgrown gardens, where the ground is fully covered but not very productive. Before there can be space to put in fresh fruitful plants some of the old ones must be dug up. Only as we continue to walk closely with the Holy Spirit can we see clearly what must go and what has to be cultivated.

Charismatic Christians who continue to move in the

Spirit have found themselves involved in the foundation of many restored churches. They have had no notion where the baptism in the Holy Spirit was going to lead them at the beginning, but today the pathway is more clearly evident, as the coming together of God's people is making it possible to harness the power poured out upon them for the benefit of the non-Christian world.

Restoration is a progressive activity in the life of the church, which will continue as long as we are submissively responsive to the slightest nudge of the Spirit and to his fresh revelations. To accomplish true restoration in every area of the church requires all Spirit-filled believers to be fully extended in their ministry, with the power of the Spirit flowing unhindered through them. Only then can we bring in the kingdom of God.

The teaching of restoration, although delivered by men, comes directly from the Spirit for the whole church, so it is no surprise that many of the denominations in our country are also reaching out for a guarded measure of restoration. Where there is a longing for the Spirit, and for growth, leadership has been prepared to abandon old set forms and institute new Spirit-led ways. The manner in which we worship and praise God has been the most obviously influenced area, but concerning other equally vital issues many seem hard of hearing. The professional 'one-man-band' type leader constitutes the biggest foot against the door to growth and restoration.

Yonggi Cho's church has until recently been affiliated to the Assemblies of God, and influenced by the United States arm of that denomination. Denominational labels are of no importance, but clogging traditions are! God will pour out his Spirit upon people who will receive it, pentecostal or otherwise; he will work where believers will co-operate.

Over the past twenty five years Yonggi Cho has been building, adapting and adjusting his church structure so that it has become a thoroughly efficient channel through which the Holy Spirit can flow. It is a modern day organisational miracle. He has had the wisdom and insight to avoid bottle-necks which would cause their growth curve to plateau. The mushrooming size of his church proves without a shadow of doubt the efficiency of the organisation that he has established. Any church, denominational or otherwise, if prepared to be radical concerning the reformation of its structure (among many other things) can experience unlimited expansion. All the Lord is looking for is a way where he can move and work.

Surely, over the past ten to fifteen years, a new heart has come into the people of God in this land. We have passed from despair and hopelessness to yearning and longing, and I believe we are now entering into yet another phase, that of expectation. What a healthy climate this has produced for the Spirit of God as he comes to work amongst us! Immediately it creates a greater readiness for change and adjustment that will make a way for God to move.

The conviction that we are preparing ourselves for a move of the Spirit in our land has been the impetus in many churches to bring all their activities, personnel and even their interpretation of the scripture to the searchlight of the Spirit and the Word. Many earnest believers, now with past faults corrected, can be tempted to spend their time titivating the house of God while waiting for the Spirit to flow down, but as we look at what God has done in Seoul we realise that there is no need to wait aimlessly for a sovereign intervention of God; there is so much we can be doing now.

'For from day to day men kept coming to David to help him, until there was a great army, like the army of God. All these, men of war, arrayed in battle order, came to Hebron with full intent to make David king over all Israel; likewise all the rest of Israel were of a single mind to make David king.' (1 Chron. 12:22, 38).

In these past years a glorious progression has been secretly taking place. Little by little the church has been moving on into God's purpose. He has been building together his army, those who have come with full intent to make Jesus king. Like David's mighty men, they have come with a single mind and have kept coming from day to day, as the great army of God. Jesus, the great David, is expected to sit upon his throne. Preparations are under way; he is calling his army together, teaching them how to keep rank and use their weapons for war, bringing them into battle formation, and leading them into complete submission to the head. This orderly army of God will be the glorious structure through which the power of God can flow; an army submitted to its head, the Lord Jesus Christ, understanding how to take instructions and carry out his will.

Prepared vessels

God's activity through the charismatic movement, followed by the upheavals over the past years, have all been part of a preparation. Previously there have been general outpourings of the Holy Spirit which have blessed the church but have not necessarily caused expansion. A new dimension has come into the thinking of many Christians for whom the personal blessing is not enough. In coming together as the army of God, men and women declare their expectation that the Spirit will come upon them collectively. They have made themselves like a prepared vessel which waits to be filled. Surely during these waiting days we should encourage our hearts because our patience is not in vain. God intends to work through his prepared people: it was his plan from the very beginning.

It has taken all these years to re-educate us, to turn the church from self-centred attitudes where we were more concerned about our personal holiness than those going to hell, and enjoying fellowship with one another in preference to evangelising our Jerusalems.

As you read of the fantastic numbers gathered into the church in Seoul, do not let unbelief stifle the anticipation in your hearts that God can do it here. Nothing is impossible to God! Why should we only expect something small? He intends to do something huge. We cannot lift our hopes and expectations too high, because there is no ceiling to what God will do for us if only we will believe.

When our hearts are gripped by the imminence of the end of the age, we will be forced to recognise that harvest-time is almost upon us.

Jesus told a parable about a man who had two kinds of plants, growing up in his field. When asked to explain it he answered, 'He who sows the good seed is the Son of man; the field is the world, and the good seed means the sons of the kingdom; the weeds are the sons of the evil one, and the enemy who sowed them is the devil; the harvest is the close of the age, and the reapers are angels. Let them both grow together until the harvest; and at harvest time I will tell the reapers, "Gather the weeds first and bind them in bundles to be burned, but gather the wheat into my barn." ' (Matt. 13:37–39, 30).

We are stepping to the edge of these things taking place. There is going to be a harvest, of the two natures; one for burning and the other for gathering into the barn of our God. But both will be a harvest to demonstrate a good return for what has been sown. God intends to gather a bumper crop, not a catastrophe like a field full of weeds with the odd stalk of corn here and there. No! There will be a bountiful return, worthy of the Lord of the harvest. To this end God has been preparing his church, intending to be honoured by a fruitful field. There will be abundance; the barn of God will be stacked high.

But before the gathering in there is work to be done. The preparation has gone deep, the plough has cut a straight furrow; we can see where we are going.

No farmer labours for nothing. While he waits for growth there is plenty for him to do, so that when the crop is cut and brought in none is lost. After his time of preparation comes to an end his activity is still purposeful, as he anticipates a good profit.

We cannot expect too much Jesus said, 'The harvest is plentiful' (Matt. 9:37). Are not these the days when the ploughmen are going to overtake the reapers? May God have a people who are willing to work in this day of his power.

God-sized churches

'So those who received his word were baptised, and there were added that day about three thousand souls' (Acts 2:41). That was how God began on the first day with his church. Small churches were never his plan, although many say, 'I don't think I would like to be in a big church; I would lose something.'

If that is true, we are trying to get that 'something' from the wrong source, or we were never intended to have it in the first place. The church on the day of Pentecost was a direct expression of God's heart. Only forty days earlier Jesus had died for the whole world. How could smallness now adequately express the magnitude of what he had done?

Somewhere along the way we have been sold a lie by the evil one, a lie that says that big churches are not really the best way of serving God's purposes on earth. That completely contradicts how God began. Big churches are a perfect means for expressing the bigness of God and the devil doesn't want us to believe that. He delights to keep a stranglehold upon the growth of the work of God by propagating the myth that small churches are best. It has been said, 'Aim at nothing, and you will be sure to hit it.' If we aim at smallness we will never grow.

It is by reading God's word that our concepts radically change: we are brought to repentance for our small restrictive attitudes towards church growth; at the same time we find our vision being enlarged, our faith raised and a new willingness within us to realign our ideas with God's.

Once we begin to see what he is really after, all manner of changes will begin to take place in the way we function to make way for a God-sized church.

Mobilise all the body

It takes a little while for the enormity of the challenge which lies ahead to soak in, but as it begins to register we will see that our only hope of successfully tackling the task is to mobilise every believer and bring them to function in the church. What God has done in the Full Gospel Central Church can happen here, but it requires every person to work, knowing that they have a commission from God to be fruitful and multiply. For this to work smoothly the leadership needs to recognise the Spirit of God in each believer, honouring his ministry and calling in them. We need to express our thankfulness to God for each person and to welcome each person's gift to the body of Christ. In this way we show our inter-dependence, and fulfil the command to submit to one another. The body requires every part to supply its own unique contribution, not excluding even the youngest.

Another reason to involve every member of the church in ministry and outreach is that each is required to be a good steward of the gifts that he has received. Within the body of the church everything necessary for its upbuilding is supplied: there are those who can pray and there are those who can witness; there are those who can care, help and give but each area of ministry must be encouraged and made accountable to God. Many an over-worked pastor could find his work alleviated if he used those with gifts and caring hearts within the fellowship. Once leaders catch the vision of the wealth God has put amongst his people, they will joyfully release these gifts to the body of Christ.

Sharing your power

Even in the church it is easy to think like the world, seeing leadership in terms of people being over or under others. But in the kingdom of God it is the exact opposite. The true leader is a servant and support, a load-bearing foundation on which the whole church can rest secure, for this God gives leaders power and authority. Yonggi Cho advises them to share their power, since to share power means to multiply it. If one man holds everything to himself capacity for growth can be stifled, and yet effective government of the local church will eventually single out one man to take final responsibility. With careful wisdom he must then share his power with other trusted leaders, and in this manner expand the base of authority. The more he is able to delegate, the larger will become the base of support in the church. It is by this means that Central Church has been able to sustain such a vast congregation. Delegation which gives real authority right down to a house group leader, caring for eight to ten families, provides a strong caring cradle to hold the whole church together.

We must have house groups

Many of those who object to large churches really do so because they fear they will lose the intimacy of close fellowship. On the day of Pentecost three thousand people suddenly became the church, meeting both all together, and house to house. It was there, in those small groups just the size of a home, that the intimacy, love, fellowship and caring took place. This is God's pattern; he has provided the big church, but knowing our needs, has given us a smaller group to which we can relate. The church in the home is God's plan. It is the answer to the 'something' we feel we will lose if we grow too large, besides giving opportunity for everybody to function in the gifts God has given them. We are not called upon to copy Yonggi Cho's style of church with home cells but we should be prepared to copy the original blueprint in the Acts of the Apostles.

It wasn't long after Pentecost before another five thousand were added to the initial three thousand. In Jerusalem the church grew so rapidly that it wasn't feasible for one person to know every other. Therefore we cannot put forth the possibility of knowing everyone as a criterion for the size of the church; instead, we need to seek God for a system of home groups which provides for the fellowship, ministry and special needs of the believers.

Every strand of a spider's web is linked into the centre, and so it should be with a cell group system. Every leader must fulfil his role submissively on behalf of the elders and leader of the church. There cannot be individualistic groups, expressing something different from the heart and ministry of the church, or the cell system would end up being divisive rather than expansive. In the Acts it was the

Apostles' doctrine that was taught house to house, not their own ideas. The unity of doctrine and submission of leader to leader produces a strong, united, vibrant body. Far from leaving the leader or pastor of the church with nothing to do, this kind of organisation can be very demanding. The home cell leaders themselves need his leadership, so that they can have confidence and security in what they teach in their groups and in how they care for the people.

What are we waiting for?

Yonggi Cho says that he could go to any city in the world and have a church of 10,000. He isn't boasting, or trying to play 'God', but intends to send a shock wave through our complacency, saying that the principles he has successfully put to work in his church will succeed anywhere in the world. Not that principles and man alone produce a church; but principles with a man empowered by the Holy Spirit will find Jesus (who builds his church) right alongside on the construction site. Do we then assume that there is not a special time when God will move by his Spirit? Or are we needlessly waiting for a supernatural intervention?

In these days we should be longing, yearning and praying, yes even fasting, that God would pour out his Spirit in such power that no one would be able to stand in his presence. God will hear our prayers and have mercy upon us as we humble ourselves to seek his face. We cannot anticipate too much. He is lavish in his mercy, and though we truly deserve nothing we can expect everything, even that which goes beyond our wildest imaginings. Although we may set our churches in order and do many right structural things in obedience to scripture, that alone cannot satisfy the hunger that God has put into the hearts of many of his people for something inconceivably glorious. They do, however, spur us on to work and co-operate in what the Spirit is showing us to do now. Yonggi Cho does not consider his present success the ultimate of what God can do; that we still wait to see. If our God came down amongst us in power, what he could accomplish in half an hour would cause our activity for the past hundred years to fade into nothingness.

While we wait with patience for the supernatural visitation of God we must not be idle as there is a measure of growth we can enjoy right now. If we will do it God's way we will experience his approval and guidance. Like the farmer, our waiting is full of activity, making ready for that day.

Time is running out

The ugly street violence that we experienced in Britain in 1981 sent a chill through the whole nation. The very fabric of our society was being torn apart and long cherished values were trampled under foot in the streets of our cities. That which non-Christians as well as Christians had held dear was being displayed to ridicule and discarded as outmoded. The 1980s offer little in the way of peace and security for the individual, or stability in the nation. Accepted norms of behaviour are being swept away; there is confusion in every area of life, where the very foundations of our society are thrown up for debate and question, but no one has an answer. The street riots indicated how close we have come to the edge of the precipice.

Showing our true colours

Something more than anxiety has sprung up in the nation as a direct result of those awful days in 1981. People's thinking has begun to polarise. Outwardly it may not yet be too evident, but as evil has become more blatant and the black has got blacker so the apathetic majority, who are the bulk of the 'don't knows' in every opinion poll, have been stirred to think and evaluate their attitudes and standards in life. On the High Street, talking to the Saturday shoppers, one senses a longing to turn the clock back and bring in old fashioned values. The moral slide in every area of society shocks them as they begin to realise how wicked wickedness can be. There is a harvest among this apathetic majority; they have been brought up short and are now prepared to consider that God could be the answer to the nation's ills. If they are to be gathered into the church speed is required, because the very nature of their infirmity means that they will all too soon allow their disturbed thoughts to drift away.

Hallelujah! God is sovereign, and through these trials and difficulties that we have experienced as a nation he has been at work, answering the prayers of his faithful ones who have cried to him day and night. Our wretched back-slidden state is becoming intolerable to more and more people in the land. Now is the time to act. We must take the gospel to the man in the street in down-to-earth communicating ways.

Christians are to be in the world but not of the world, a balance which many have found difficult, with the result that the majority live as if they had cotton wool in their ears and a blind-fold around their eyes, trying to pretend nothing has happened. God allowed us to come up to the precipice edge and to take a good hard look. It is his people in this land who are responsible for the direction we take, not the government or anyone else. Either we end up in revolution and anarchy, or by the grace of God we can turn ourselves and the nation about to receive mercy in a mighty outpouring of the Holy Spirit.

The process of birth has begun

At the same time that Satan has been so busy in the world, God has been very active in his church. All over the land an anticipation for something glorious has been sown supernaturally in people's hearts. We believe the end will not be revolution, not because we don't deserve it, but because our God is so merciful, and has heard and is beginning to answer the prayers of his people. In the same way as Yonggi Cho incubates his dreams and visions until they come into being, thousands of Christians have reached out in believing faith to possess a mighty revival, to bring in the kingdom of God and his rule of righteousness in the land.

In the fulness of time God sent forth his Son to be born

of Mary. The time of preparation was complete; God had spoken his word into the heart of one simple woman and shared it with his prophets, Anna and Simeon. Once the word was spoken and received, a process began which nothing could stop. Inexorably the babe grew in Mary's womb, filling every corner of it. She could not stop him being born, or speed up his arrival; at God's appointed time the birth took place. Don't you feel a tingling in your bones? the word has been spoken to us, has taken deep root, is now growing. There's nothing that can stop it; it will bear fruit. God's prophets have received and proclaimed his word. Already the process has begun and the birth will surely take place.

In the same way as a mother makes preparation for the babe that is going to be born, God has been busy with his preparations. He has sent his word into the hearts of his prophets and given them the ability to speak it in such a way as to lead the people to anticipate the glory which is about to come upon them.

Anticipation

The only words of anticipation the prophets dare to speak to the church are those they have heard directly from God, who has promised to share his secrets with them so that they can then declare them to his people. Anticipation of what God is going to do is a powerful means of promoting and encouraging our faith, so that the whole body of Christ gets involved with the vision. It will give us new eyes with which to view the world in its sick state, keeping us from being dragged into its despair, or being sold its fatalistic attitudes by the evil one. The prophets' word encouraging us to expect God's intervention confirms our hearts in the assurance that Christ is the only answer to our chaotic world.

Preparation

As the prophets stir our imagination to take hold of the wonders that God is about to do, we all need to make ready. Now is the time to prepare. First we should all wait and be baptised in the Holy Spirit, making ourselves totally available to God, to do his will. Each of us has only one life and in that short spell of time let us aspire to be responsible citizens of the kingdom of God, who minister his authority upon earth and serve our generation. The opportunity now is ours; what follows is somebody else's responsibility.

Next our attention should be directed to cleansing the church; the clutter of law and tradition which militates against the Spirit of God must all be cleared out. If hundreds of thousands are going to be gathered into the church we need to do some clear thinking, and to prepare the foundations which must be adequate to carry the load to be put upon them.

The elders, the pillars of the church must be stable, pure and upright, when measured against the plumbline of God. If open sin cannot tempt a man Satan, who is an expert in these things, prepares other subtle measures. As our churches grow the temptation to build personal empires will become the greater. Faithfulness and loyalty, two beautiful qualities, will come under attack because they are part of the foundation for unity and thus for growth. Full Gospel Central Church is not the only large church in Seoul; Young Nak Presbyterian Church has 50,000 in its congregation and other large churches successfully function without fear of tearing apart into splinters and divisions. Death to self-seeking and a willingness among all levels of leadership to submit humbly one to another are both necessary for the development of large churches.

Are we too rich?

In recent years God has poured out his Holy Spirit mainly among poor communities: South America and Indonesia, the tribal areas of India, Cambodia and Korea. Can the prosperous West not qualify for the blessing of God, or is it only for the poor?

Certainly in our western society we have too many alternatives to God. With a welfare state providing doctors and psychiatrists for the sick in body and mind; sociologists and economists providing a satisfactory appeal to the clever; the rational West has devised an answer or suggested a reason for everything and by so doing we have pushed God so low on our priorities that we have almost disqualified ourselves from his intervention.

The bible says, 'How hard it is for a rich man to enter into the kingdom of God.' The West is rich and our riches, by providing alternatives to God, have hardened our hearts. Investments, bank balances and regular incomes easily become our security, rather than trusting God. Most 'middle class' people wouldn't consider themsleves to be particularly rich, but they are rich enough to falsely trust their own resources. It has been said, 'When confronted with death, all men are believers; when confronted with want all wish there was a God.' The riches of our society have ensnared us in unbelief, and our hearts have embraced the love of money, so that it has become hard to enter the kingdom of God. We have transferred our root of security from God to our ability to be our own saviour.

Do we have to suffer?

Were the decades of suffering experienced by Korea one of the means of preparation God used before he sent revival? Suffering is a common feature in the places where God's Spirit has been poured out in these past few years and it does appear to have prepared the way, turning people to God. Although everything hasn't been painless for us as a nation, we have been spared the horrors that many have had to endure, living a relatively peaceful life compared with many parts of the world. If suffering in that extreme measure was a requirement for the blessings of God, then at that point we would fail. But this is not so, because there is nothing meritorious in suffering of itself; by it we cannot earn, or qualify for, God's mercy. But there is a suffering to which we must be introduced if we are to see a break-through in our land. Paul writes, '. . . that I may know him and the power of his resurrection, and may share his sufferings, becoming like him in his death . . .' (Phil. 3:10).

Although Jesus suffered cruelly in his physical body, his heart was the true centre of all his anguish. Because he loved so much his heart was broken, torn apart by his own wayward, sin-loving creation. He let his heart run out after them, calling them in their rebellion to come. He only wanted them to turn and to load their sin upon himself, which he knew would mean his death.

The heart of Jesus bears an invitation, which few care to notice, to come right in and share his sufferings. It is not a pleasant place to enter. To pass through the door we have to die. But there we can intimately learn to know him and the power of his resurrection, as we allow his painful wounded heart to close around us in a fellowship to which nothing can compare. We shall feel his heart beat for this hell-bound world and no longer will we be satisfied with anything less than a life wholly sacrificed to burn for him.

Praise God, he hasn't set any level of physical suffering which has to be endured before he will turn and have mercy upon us as a people, but he has set us a life and death option, so that by choice we too can qualify for God's moving among us.

Be an hilarious giver

The prescription God gives to rich men who want to enter into the kingdom of God touches their hearts first and then their pockets. Of course it is possible for us in our rich western societies to enjoy the blessing of God in the same way as experienced in many less privileged areas of the world. Covetousness, greed and the love of money, a triple-headed monster, must first be ruled out of our hearts. It is joy to expel these sins and then like little children come to trust our loving heavenly Father. A heart of trust and dependency, looking to God for all of our sufficiency, fosters genuine faith. Once our hearts have been thoroughly dealt with, the next stage to spiritual health requires a delight in giving so that we become those cheerful givers that the bible talks about and God loves. In the end it does not matter how much or how little we have, but whether we are identified with the big giving heart of our God. Only then can we enter into his blessings.

It may seem strange, but to qualify for God's blessing it is important that we are liberated to give. The regular honouring of God with our tithes and offerings is the most simple tangible way in which we can express our total dependence upon him. Amid the clutter of our electrical applicances, house extensions and new cars we can walk joyfully as true heavenly pilgrims. Our western lifestyle does not need to be a weight upon us, God can work in this kind of society as effectively as anywhere else. It is not our society or way of life that prohibits us entering into the blessing, it is only a matter of our hearts. As Christians we can get our possessions into perspective and with thankful hearts we can enjoy them. Many of the sophistications of our life can actually become tools by which we can more effectively serve the kingdom. God has not called us to live some frugal life of asceticism in the midst of our western plenty but rather to align our hearts and behaviour with his individual will for each of us.

Ready learners

There are few places in the world where missionaries have not ventured, and in the past Britain was at the forefront of foreign missionary endeavour. Thousands of dedicated men and women have given their lives to see the nations turn to Christ; they were teachers for the whole world. But now we are the ones who sit in need of learning. It is our turn to be challenged by powerful teachers. Every student requires a humble heart if he is going to learn, and God is providing us with that opportunity. The onus is now upon us to admit our need and meekly to learn, recognising our new teachers.

The magnificent work that God has done in Full Gospel Central Church is not necessarily there for us to copy in each detail, but we will never see the blessing that they have received unless we express the same spirit and desire. God hasn't any favourites but he does have principles by which he works, and it is those who obey them who receive the blessings.

The most extravagant visions of God's power moving across our land are all in the realm of possibility. We could see it with our eyes and delight in it if we would learn what God is saying to us. May a humble, teachable spirit come upon the church of God, to motivate us to implement the principles laid out for all to see in the sign that God has raised up. It is written clearly, as if in large words on a blackboard, so we can understand what it is we have to do. There may not be many men of the calibre of Yonggi Cho, but I believe there are those prepared to enter God's school of training. With the right leaders we can have mighty churches in our land, held together in the unity of the Spirit and overflowing with God's blessing, as he commands it to rest where brothers dwell together in unity.

The costly example of praying that has been held up before us is not just for our admiration but so that we also should enter into that school of training and learn how to pull down the strongholds of wickedness that have held our nation captive for years. By our prayers we can throw back the threat of anarchy, and rescue our nation from the edge of calamity. As we win the battle in the heavenlies, captives will be loosed on earth and the chains of bondage will be broken. The trumpet call has been sounded. Now is the time for us to act. We must become co-workers with God in the secret place. He has spoken his word, a conception has taken place, and right now it grows, soon to burst forth; now is the time to pray and make ready.

Scattered across the churches of our land are men equipped to lead because they have first aspired to be learners. Seek out such men who are determined to go the way of the Spirit, those who have caught the vision, join yourself to them. They are the leaders for the army of God which is coming together. God does not necessarily tell us all what he is going to do. Most of us are followers, and need these men who have heard God and are going in the right direction.

Some people will need to move into new churches so

that they can identify themselves with what God is doing in our land. The army of God is drawing together, it is not one of individuals with their own ideas and their own plans of action, but a related company of people who have submitted themselves to the leadership of Christ as he has ordained it in their local church.

Pulling back the curtain

It is the prophets' privilege to peep beyond the curtain of the present so that by their insight the church can prepare for the future. God sent John the Baptist to prepare the way for Jesus at his first coming. Before his birth, Gabriel visited his father, Zechariah, to take him the good news that his wife Elizabeth, although barren, was to conceive. Becauze Zechariah was unable to believe, he became dumb till after John's birth. That did not hinder the purpose of God. Elizabeth still conceived and produced a child. There are prophets today who would be better dumb than speaking unbelief at a time when God is speaking faith by his prophets who continue in the spirit of Elijah, preparing the way of the Lord in our generation. God's prophets are the ones who have been commissioned with the ministry to initiate restoration so that Jesus can return.

The bible says, 'Heaven must receive Jesus until the period of restoration of all things about which God spoke by the mouth of his holy prophets from ancient time' (Acts 3:20, 21). He will not return until all is complete. For this reason many leaders in our land have set themselves to work for restoration. It has put life into our services on a Sunday and led to more radical changes than just the hymn books. In places it has meant the painful task of setting aside unsuitable elders.

Anna the prophetess was able to share heaven's joyful anticipation of the birth of Jesus. She was allowed to be on the inside of God's eternal plan of redemption. Continually she was found in the temple. She had heard the word, so she worshipped God for his matchless grace, fasting and praying night and day to bring it to pass. In many of today's churches there are prophets with a similar ministry which is developing and expanding. They burn with the vision that God has allowed them to behold and worship him for the sure thing he is going to do. They too are learning to fast and pray to bring their vision into being. It completely takes hold of their expectations for the future. They know what God is saying and it is as sure to them as tomorrow's sunrise. Naturally it has fundamentally influenced their teaching; what they have seen in the dark they are revealing in the light. The vision is being broken down and given to the people little by little so that their hearts can be expanded and caught with its thrill.

What God has begun he is surely going to finish. Already the wheels are set in motion, restoration is underway, the vessel is being prepared to accommodate the expected deluge of God's Spirit. We look for Jesus to come, but first there will be harvest. All the nations are going to be reaped, including our own. The prophets are the forerunners, with the audacity to say, 'It's going to pour with rain', when not a drop has been seen for years. They have noted the cloud as small as a man's hand.

Today's prophet is not solitary like a bird on a roof, but part of a team with the apostle, evangelist, pastor and teacher; together they work out in the whole life of the church the word that has been revealed. When God has given us such opportunity, how essential it is that we get involved where the prophetic word is being fulfilled. God speaks with the intention that his word should be worked out by the whole church. The onus is upon us to set our hearts to follow.

Cho claims that he could have a church of ten thousand in any city of the world, 'Not because I am particularly clever, or educated; I am just dependent upon the Holy Spirit.' In the same way, using the advice and wisdom of Cho's years of experience, and by the power of the Spirit, it is equally possible for God to do it here.

In 1977 Dr Cho went to Australia for a church growth seminar. At about the same time, the Lord spoke to the Rev Houston who was then the General Superintendent for the Assemblies of God in the Netherlands and also the

President of their bible college. In a vision he was told to go to Sydney and begin a new church. Six months later with only nine adults the new venture began and now, within three short years, the church has exploded into 1,700 and still grows apace. The Rev Houston was a man sent by God, anointed by the Spirit, possessing a clear understanding of how to build. There is no reason why God shouldn't do exactly the same here.

It is one thing for the apostles and prophets in our churches to see these things and long for them to take place, but quite another for them actually to materialise.

With this burden upon his heart, my husband, Alan, looked out across the congregation and wondered how God was ever going to bring in the ten thousand he had been promised. The burden alone could not produce it, but as he stood before the people, ordinary mums and dads with their family responsibilities and eager young people who were busy with their studies, he knew that the miracle would come through them.

When Abraham stood with God and viewed the land to the east, the west, the north and the south it was almost laughable for him to think that he would ever possess and populate it. He was childless, both he and Sarah his wife were old, and yet God said to him, 'Through you shall all the families of the earth be blessed.'

It was some time before Abraham found faith for the child he was promised, but even then he was still powerless to produce it; Sarah also had to come to faith. She was the one who would bring the miracle to birth.

Looking at the congregation before him, Alan saw them as his Sarah who had to receive faith that impossibilities were possible to very ordinary persons like themselves.

When he first talked about an army of ten thousand in our district few could really believe. In time the idea has grown, so that now they are not laughing with unbelief like Sarah did at first, but are eager to prepare themselves in faith to be the means by which God can gather in his harvest in our locality.

The church is growing. Our numbers are doubling each

year, but even one thousand still seems a long way away. We have a lot to learn, deep wells of prayer yet to explore and new heights of faith to attain. But something has been quickened in our hearts, a 'knowing' has been conceived and we are cast on God to see it come forth. We look with expectancy for a miracle.

When the Lord brought back the captives to Zion,
We were like men who dreamed.
Our mouths were filled with laughter,
Our tongues with songs of joy.
Then it was said among the nations,
'The Lord has done great things for them.'
The Lord has done great things for us,
And we are filled with joy.
Restore our fortunes, O Lord,
Like streams in the Negev.
Those who sow in tears will reap with songs of joy.
He who goes out weeping, carrying seed to sow,
Will return with songs of joy, carrying sheaves with him.

(Ps. 126, NIV)

References

CHAPTER 1

1. F. Bartleman, 'Asouza Street' (Logos International)
2. R. Mouod, 'The Korean Revival' (Hodder & Stoughton) p. 26
3. Dan. 3:17, 25

CHAPTER 3

1. 'Redemption Tidings', 18th June, 1981
2. See 1 Chron. 12:22, 38
3. Heb. 11:6

CHAPTER 5

1. 'Answers to Life's Dilemmas', World of Faith Special Issue 1981 (Full Gospel Central Church)
2. See Phil. 4:19
3. Rom. 8:31
4. See Acts 19:2
5. 'The Mighty Advance of the Gospel', World of Faith Special Issue 1981 (Full Gospel Central Church)

CHAPTER 6

1. See Matt. 6:33
2. See 1 Peter 5:7
3. See 2 Tim. 1:7
4. See Phil. 4:13
5. See Rom. 8:37
6. See Mark 16:15

CHAPTER 7

1. Acts 2:17, 19
2. John 2:11
3. Luke 2:12

CHAPTER 8

1. See John 4:35

Bibliography

It has not always been easy to give credit to the sources of material used in this book, as the story of the Full Gospel Central Church is repeated in many books and articles, together with Dr Cho's personal testimony, which is available in parts, on various tapes and frequently referred to in his preaching. What I have recorded, is gleaned from all these sources. A list of helpful books follows:

Light of the East, and Insight into Korea
Ed. In-Hah Jung
Pub. Sahmbo Publishing Corp. Seoul
c. March 1972

Korea and its Christianity
Spencer J. Palmer
Pub. Hollym Corp. Seoul
c. 1967

Wild Fire: Church Growth in Korea
Roy E. Shearer
Pub. Eerdmans Publishing Company
Michigan Grand Rapids
c. 1966

Korea Insights
Ed. Jeon Kyu Tae
Pub. Sejong Corporation, Seoul
c. 1974

The Passing of Korea
Homer B. Hulbert
Pub. Yonsei University Press, Seoul
c. 1969

The Scrutible Oriental
Hugh MacMahon
Pub. Sejong Corporation, Seoul
c. 1975

Dream Your Way to Success
Nell L. Kennedy
Pub. Logos International
c. 1980

Successful Home Cell Groups
Dr Paul Yonggi Cho
Pub. Logos International
c. 1981

The Fourth Dimension
Dr Paul Yonggi Cho
Pub. Logos International
c. 1979

Caught in the Web
John and Karen Hurston
Pub. Church Growth International
c. 1977

Appendix 1: Map

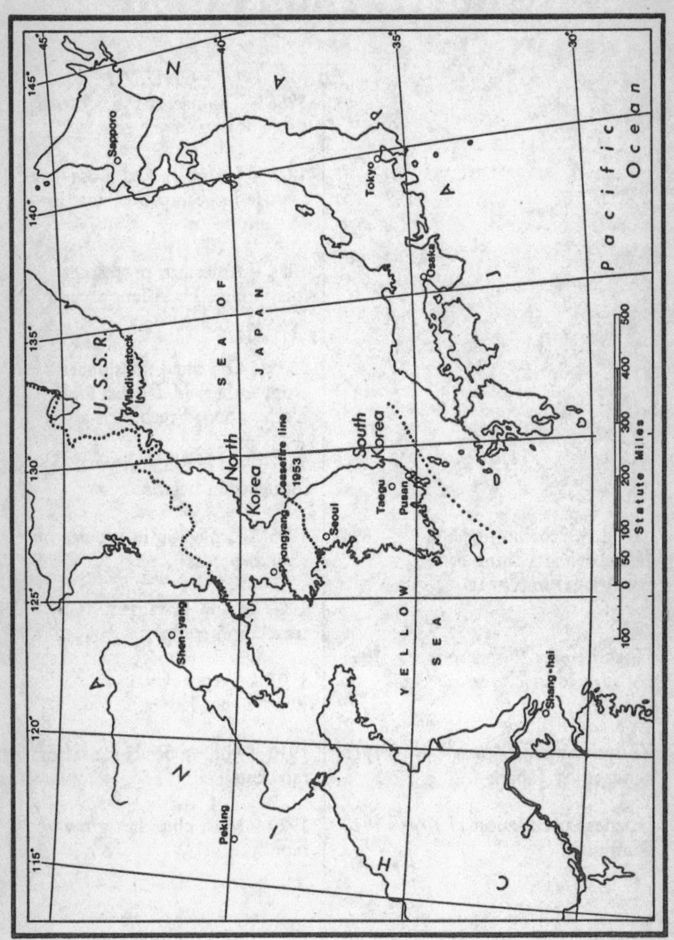

Appendix 2:
Comparison of events in Church and Nation

NATION	*YEAR*	*CHURCH*
		1866 – Thomas of the Scottish Bible Society martyred
		1876 – McIntyre and Rose baptise Korean protestants in Manchuria
		1884 – American protestant missionary, Dr Allen, arrives in Korea.
		1885 – Ordained missionaries Appenseller, Methodist and Underwood, Presb. arrive.
		1887 – Wide missionary intineration begins
Tonghak rebellion occurs. Japan defeats China in war partly held in Korea	1894	1895 – Explosion in growth of church occurs.
		1900 – New Testament translation complete
Japan defeats Russia in war partly held in Korea	1904	
		1907 – Great revival in Pyongyang, Korea.
Yi dynasty fell. Korea annexed by Japan.	1910	1910 – Million Souls for Christ movement
Japanese occupation of Korea continues	1920	1920 – Most churches grow rapidly.

		1938 – Church membership begins to decline through Japanese persecution.
Japanese involvement in World War II	1941	
Korea 'liberated' to Russia in north and USA in south. Republic of Korea founded, Refugees move into south.	1945	
Communist invasion in Korea	1950	
Armistice agreement complete	1953	1953 – Churches again rapidly grow.
		1954 – Reconsturction and relief funds pour into Korean churches
Military revolution	1961	1961 – Good church growth as church co-operates with government.
		1965 – Evangelisation of Nation by Crusade with Billy Graham and Bill Wright.
President Park assinated	1980	
		1981 – Evangelistic crusade of Plaza – three million heard gospel daily for seven days. 20,000 added to the church.
		1984 – Centenary of first resident protestant missionaries.

Appendix 3: How the church evolved

1958 – First tent church – Taejo Dong (outskirts of Seoul)

1961 – Move to West Gate, Sodaemoon, a building seating 1,500 and called Full Gospel Revival Centre

1962 – Changed name to Full Gospel Central Church

1964 – Added a balcony to seat 500

1967 – Five storey front built. Home cell system started with lay leaders and pastoral staff added.

1969 – Ground breaking ceremony on a new site in Yoido, government district of Seoul. Now 8,000 members.

1972 – Central Church sent out first missionaries. Korean fellowships set up in North and South America, Asia and Europe.

1973 – Prayer Mountain established by Pastor Jashil Choi. New Yoido church dedicated with 10,000 seats.

1974 – Total of 20,000 members. Within two years a network of more than 1,500 home cells had grown.

1977 – Ten storey World Mission Centre dedicated. Memorial Gym and auxiliary chapels built to cater for the overflow by using closed-circuit television.

1981 – Construction of New World Mission Centre began.

1981 – Membership reached 200,000, 200 ministers – two Wednesday mid-week meetings, Sunday services at 7 a.m., 9 a.m., 11 a.m., 1 p.m., 5 p.m., and 7 p.m.

1982 – Main auditorium to be expanded to seat 25,000

1984 – 500,000 faith goal

Appendix 4: Organisational Structure of

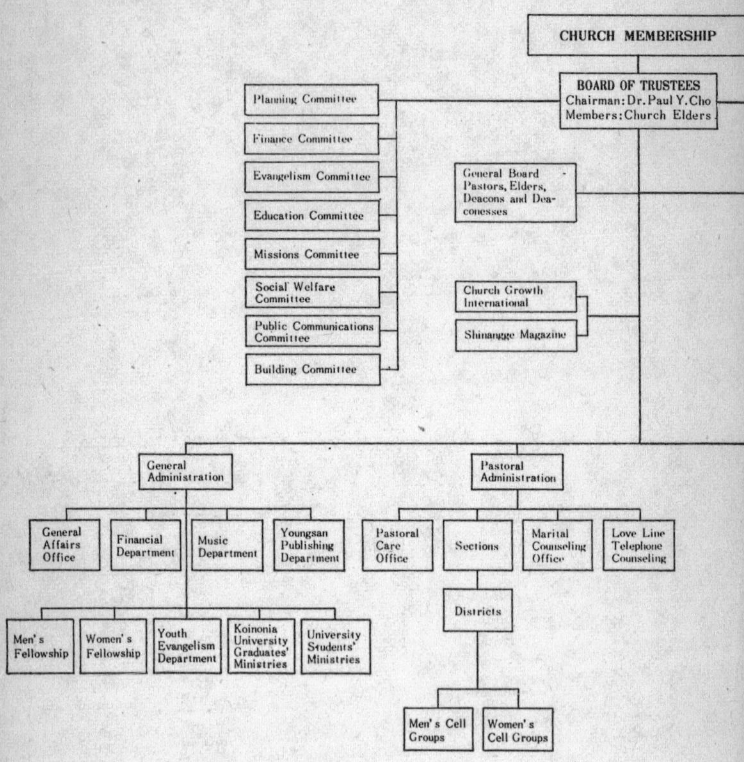

Full Gospel Central Church

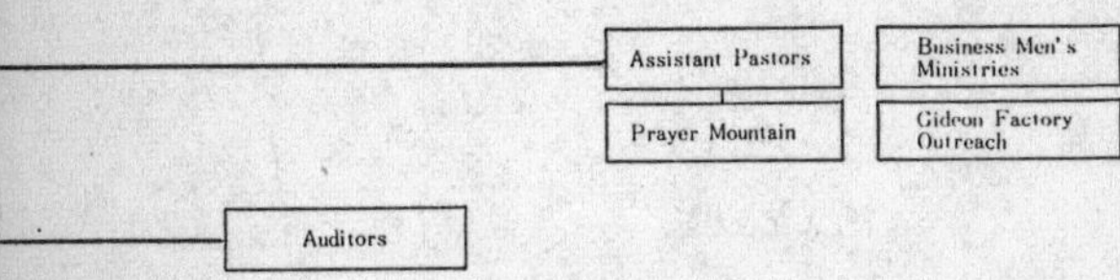

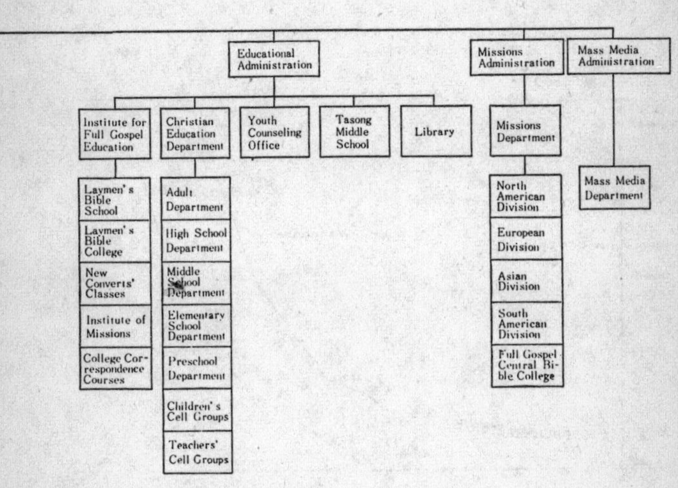

Appendix 5: Graph of Church growth

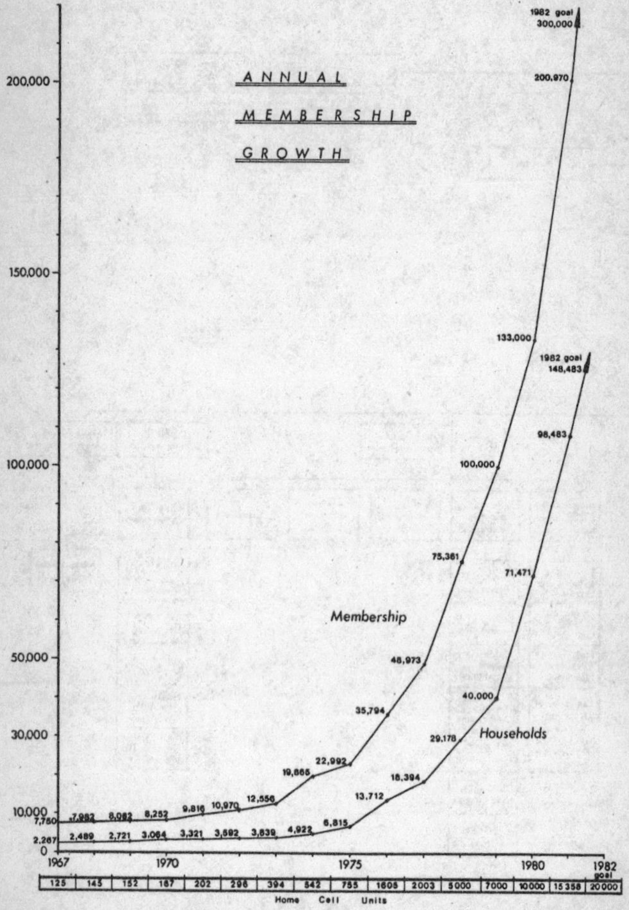

Appendix 6:
Seoul city cell system plan

Map of Seoul Divided into 12 Home Cell Units

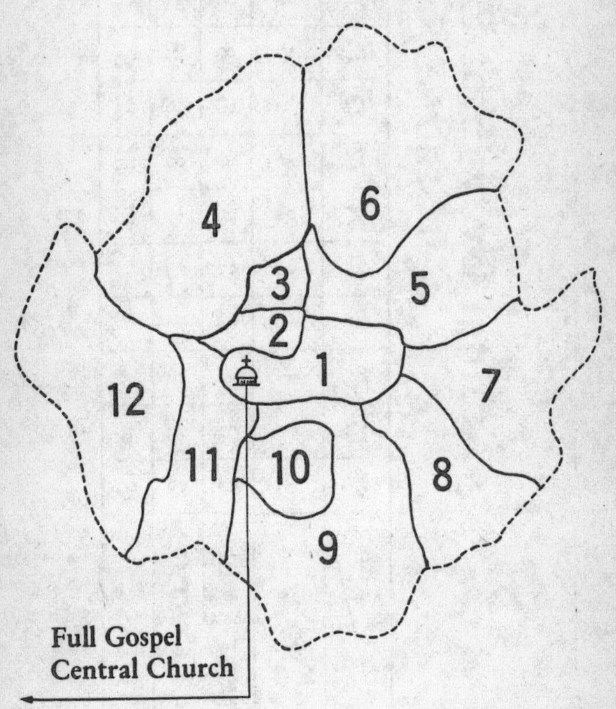

Annual Growth of Pastoral Staff

ITEM \ YEAR		66	67	68	69	70	71	72	73	74	75	76	77	78	79	80	81
ORDAINED PASTOR		1	1	1	1	2	2	4	4	8	8	8	10	12	13	14	22
LICENSED PASTOR	MEN	0	0	1	2	2	5	6	7	8	9	14	21	28	33	53	93
	WOMEN	2	2	2	2	2	4	3	9	16	28	35	47	55	68	78	154
TOTAL		3	3	4	5	6	11	13	20	32	45	57	78	95	114	145	269

Appendix 7: Pastoral Structure Diagram

DR CHO

PASTORAL
CARE DIRECTOR

CENTRAL SECRETARY

DISTRICT HEADS

SECTION HEADS

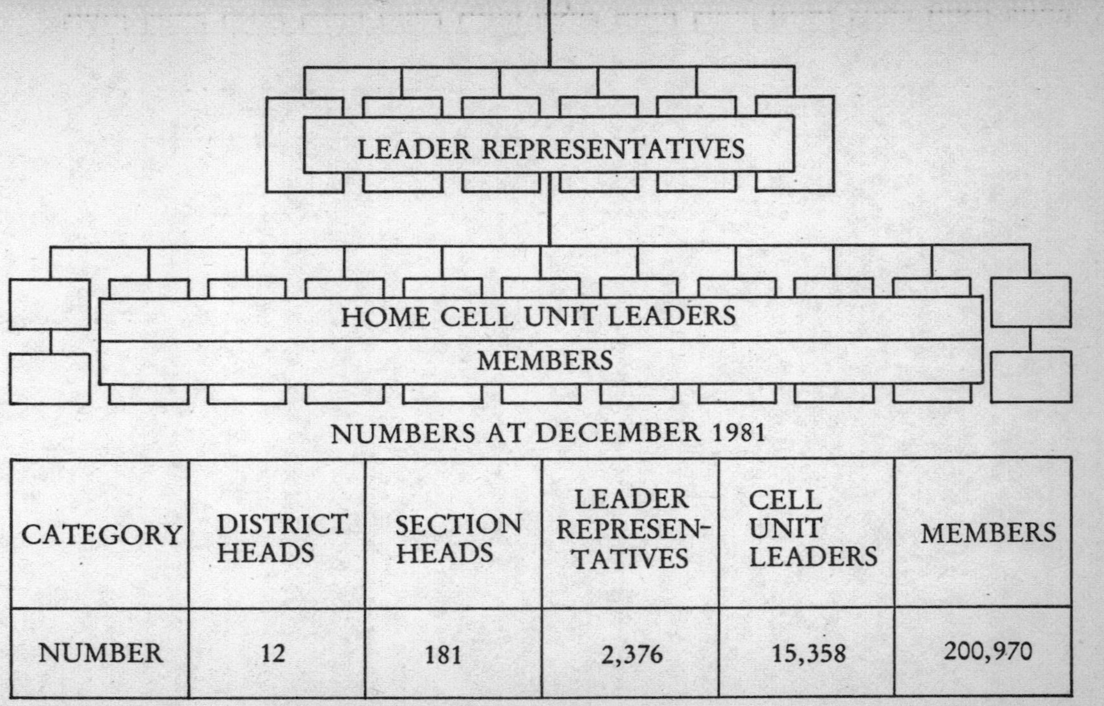

NUMBERS AT DECEMBER 1981

CATEGORY	DISTRICT HEADS	SECTION HEADS	LEADER REPRESEN-TATIVES	CELL UNIT LEADERS	MEMBERS
NUMBER	12	181	2,376	15,358	200,970